RELIGION IN SOCIAL CONTEXT:
Tradition and Transition

Consulting Editor:
CHARLES H. PAGE,
University of Massachusetts

RELIGION IN SOCIAL CONTEXT

Tradition and Transition

N. J. DEMERATH III
and **PHILLIP E. HAMMOND**
University of Wisconsin

Random House   New York

to Charles Y. Glock

CONTENTS

RELIGION IN SOCIAL CONTEXT:
Tradition and Transition

INTRODUCTION

*What to a theologian is valuable in his religion cannot play
a very large part in this study. We are concerned with what, from
a religious point of view, are often quite superficial and unrefined
aspects of religious life, but which, and precisely because they
were superficial and unrefined, have often influenced
outward behavior most profoundly.*

—MAX WEBER
The Protestant Ethic and
the Spirit of Capitalism (1928)

If, as someone has said, an expert is a fool away from home,
then any expert whose various homes include theology, history, philosophy, and anthropology as well as sociology is
always apt to be away from one home or another and hence
especially vulnerable to the charge. Students of religion can
hardly remain aloof to any of these disciplines, though
knowledge in any one of them may require a career of
preparation. It is with willing trepidation, therefore, that we
offer the present volume as a *sociological* treatment of a

subject that many have treated in other ways. Not an apology, the statement is merely meant modestly to follow Max Weber's own path.

The sociological analysis of religion has four distinctive characteristics worth identifying here. First, its concepts have empirical referents. This distinguishes it from theology; indeed, if the theology of religion is "knowledge of God," then the sociology of religion is in part "knowledge of those who seek knowledge of God." Second, sociology attempts rigorous abstraction from the particular to the general. This distinguishes it in some measure from history. Where the history of religion often focuses on particular persons or events for their own sake, the sociology of religion views these persons and events as instances of more general phenomena. Although much of this volume will be given over to historical data, they are offered to exemplify concepts of wider utility. A third difference is related to the second: our interest is chiefly in socially structured or group behavior rather than in individuals or the psychology of religion. In some cases this means merely a concern for "national" trends rather than for the tendencies of particular persons, but in all cases it means attention to those features of social behavior that obtain regardless of the unique attributes of the persons involved. Thus, analysis of church organization reveals that in the "episcopal" form of hierarchy the local clergy behave differently from their counterparts in a "congregational" structure and do so irrespective of who those clergy happen to be. Far from denying the authenticity of personal impress or the importance of individual character, the sociological point of view holds simply that such individual differences are acted out within contexts that are themselves influential and amenable to analysis.

Finally, a fourth distinctive characteristic of the sociological approach to religion is that it seeks to relate religion to other facets of social experience. Along with family life, religion is among the few institutional spheres in which almost everyone participates in some way from childhood, making it a crucible for testing one's objectivity and giving it a manifold relevance to the cumulative affairs of man, especially when religion is defined sociologically rather than theologically. Insofar as it concerns beliefs, values, rituals, organizational processes, and a changing societal fabric, religion's elements operate both in the conventional church and in virtually every other nook and cranny of society, including the formally "nonreligious." The religious experience need not be confined to the otherworldly, the mystical, or, of course, the Biblical. It is precisely because analytic elements of that experience are crucial to social life generally that the experience itself engages our attention. Indeed, the sociology of religion is confined if we must analyze religion in its own terms alone. Not only does the study of religion have implications for the study of politics, education, and so forth, but the study of religion can itself be enhanced by concepts drawn from, say, political sociology and the sociology of education.

Throughout, the book's major objective is to give brief coherence to an area of sociology known more for its disparate—one might even say "schizophrenic"—character than for its unity. For the sociology of religion is both heir to the grandest theoretical tradition in all of sociology and perpetrator of some of its most sterile research. "Sterile" is used advisedly. It is not that empirical investigations of religion are so bad; rather, they have been largely irrelevant to the theoretical questions behind them. Thus, instructors of the sociology of religion often find themselves teaching two courses: one dealing with the grand tradition and its issues of religious development, the moral basis of society, the role of symbols in human behavior, and so forth; the other reporting study after study of church attendance, the role conflict of the minister, and rates of belief in God. We exaggerate, but only a little. From our own experience in teaching such a course, we realized that what are needed are conceptual bridges capable of articulating such lofty theories and mundane regularities. As an example, a later discussion of patterns and problems in religious organization uses several concepts from secular organizational analysis to bring together, on the one hand, global theoretical judgments concerning the importance of normative systems in society and the possibility of normative deviance and, on the other hand, statistical analysis of individual beliefs and rates of church participation.

The book comprises six chapters divided into two equal parts. The initial three chapters deal almost entirely with the classical literature in the sociology of religion, with the first devoted to men like Emile Durkheim, Sigmund Freud, Edward Tylor, and F. Max Müller in the "primitive materials tradition" and the next two devoted to much closer analysis of a single scholar, Max Weber. Throughout this part, our objective is not only to savor but to criticize, for many of these writers are important for the enormity of their errors as well as the brilliance of their insights. Moreover, we have sought to avoid an appreciation of these men as museum pieces whose age alone commands respect. Each of them raised issues of contemporary relevance; each of them contributed to the basic framework of the sociology of religion as it now confronts the current religious scene. But why should Weber as only one individual preempt so very much of so short a book? The answer, in our view, is threefold. First, we feel that even a short book should pick a point at which to sacrifice breadth for depth; we thought it worthwhile to devote at least a part of the volume to a more detailed treatment of a single individual. Second, Weber qualifies as a seminal giant who, like no other figure, straddles both the past and the current enterprise of the sociology of religion. Finally, Weber's work, especially *The Protestant Ethic and the Spirit of Capitalism,* has occupied a large number of other scholars in its wake and has produced some of the most far-reaching debates concerning the basic issues of "religion in social context."

The second part of the book addresses contemporary American religion more specifically, though it frequently relies upon concepts developed in the first part. Chapter IV concerns a host of theoretical and methodological questions concerning the individual and his religion. Chapter V deals with religious organizations. Chapter VI asks about the relationships between religion and society at large. Actually, this last chapter is the most wide-ranging and serves as a summary in drawing upon elements of all five of the preceding chapters. After all, one certainly cannot understand religion's relationship to society without first understanding something about religion in other societies—whether primitive or European from the first century through the Reformation. Then, too, it is difficult to fathom the role of religion in society without calling upon certain assumptions about individual religiosity and the internal dynamics of church organization.

If all these chapters appear pessimistic, attending more to religion's problems than to its aspirations, our only defense is that we have written that way knowingly. In part this approach is used because the search for problems is a good analytic device if one seeks to examine how any institution really works, but it is also because religion is, in fact, in a currently problematic position in our society. Indeed, for this very reason, its sociological study can be a fascinating venture.

Insofar as this volume is a textbook, then, it departs from the conventional. For one thing, it is considerably shorter than most texts. It eschews any exhaustive cataloging either of the available literature or of the manifold ideas generally in the field; it seeks instead to focus on particularly pivotal literature and ideas. Nor is the book intended merely to lay out elementary notions. In every field, poor or outworn axioms are perpetuated by uncritical texts; this one instead attempts to grapple with new and challenging insights so as to stimulate further thinking. It is our conviction that most students and most readers can appreciate criticism and innovation as part of the learning experience itself.

For all these reasons, the book's utility may differ from that of most texts in several ways. First, it may serve as an introduction to the field for those who have very little knowledge of it but want a point of beginning and an invitation to further study. This audience is especially appealing not only because of our missionary impulse on behalf of sociology itself, but also because we would share the excitement that comes from fresh views of familiar phenomena. In this spirit the book might serve as a quick, initial reading assignment in a course on the sociology of religion to afford a preview of what is to come; or it might serve as the "religious" reading in an introductory course that assigns one paperback per topic. A second use is more traditionally textlike. Although the volume would be inadequate as the sole reading in any course devoted entirely to the sociology of religion, it could serve as supplementary reading throughout the course, offering brief interpretations and critiques of original sources. A third use is for the advanced student and the professional. We have already mentioned that the book was not written as a condescending primer. Although it is designed for the sophisticated beginner, it also raises issues and advances perspectives that we hope the expert himself will find arresting. In our view sociology presents no necessary incompatibility between writing simultaneously for beginners and for experts. Although their reactions may occur at different levels, reaction itself is the crucial thing.

Finally, we have a roster of acknowledgments that defies any complete listing, partly because it includes a number of students whose names we have forgotten but who reacted meaningfully to various portions of the manuscript, either in draft form or as unwritten lectures in our courses. Several of our colleagues have also lent a helpful critical hand, particularly Anthony Costonis and Charles Perrow. And yet our dedication is meant to acknowledge the volume's greatest debt, to Charles Y. Glock. Happily, he taught at Columbia before going to Berkeley, so both of us could benefit from him as teacher and friend even though we pursued graduate studies a country apart. Of course, many serve their students as good teachers and good friends, but only a few confront challenging issues with conscientious discipline, providing a personal example that endures beyond the graduate school experience. Glock is one of those few.

N. J. Demerath III *and* Phillip E. Hammond

Madison, Wisconsin

PART ONE

*History and the Conceptual Development
of the Sociology of Religion*

I

THE PRIMITIVE MATERIALS TRADITION:
Early Questions and Early Answers

Of the many strands out of which contemporary sociology of religion is woven, few are as marked as the "primitive materials" tradition. Of course, numerous scholars have turned perceptive attention to religion from a variety of stances. But when social science was an infant, evolutionism dominated much of Western thought, and it was natural, therefore, for early social scientists to turn to primitive man, believing that the rudiments of social life could be discovered in "rudimentary" societies. Emile Durkheim, many of his predecessors, and some of his successors followed just such a strategy, and the sociology of religion is richer because they did. In this chapter we shall discover how rich this heritage is. In our assessment we shall be concerned, however, not only with the viability of their answers but also, and more importantly, with the viability of their questions.

Primitive societies, in many respects, *are* simple. Typically they are small in population, condensed in geography, uncomplicated in economics, and little differentiated in politics. Homogeneous in many ways that modern societies are heterogeneous, primitive societies are generally preliterate and also slow to change. Thus, they were especially attractive to the social scientist who would discover in them the roots of modern social life. Of course, we now know that only a naïve and chauvinistic evolutionism would posit unilinear, inevitable "progress." But even without this latter-day sophistication, the early social scientists arrived at valuable insights into many spheres of life, and the sphere of religion was no exception.

In pursuit of their insights into religion, the present chapter has four sections. It begins by reviewing the work of two early anthropologists, Sir Edward Tylor and F. Max Müller, who viewed evolutionism as the development of increasing knowledge and saw early religion as a stopgap for inadequate explanations of nature and man's role in it. The second section turns to Sigmund Freud and an evolutionism based on emotional rather than intellectual development; Freud portrayed early religion as the result more of psychoanalytic confusion than of cognitive error. Still another brand of evolutionism occupies the third section, a brand based upon sociological factors rather than on either individual intellect or emotions. Emile Durkheim, a giant in sociology generally, figures prominently here. Finally, the fourth section summarizes and synthesizes the previous materials. It ends with brief mention of several recent analyses of primitive religion to indicate that primitive materials are still relevant, especially when the yoke of naïve evolutionism is cast off.

Animism and Naturism: The Mystique of Mistakes

℞ One of the early theoretical insights has come to be known as animism, the point of view that sees religion as an explanation for "spirits." Each of us dreams, sees his reflection in quiet water, and has periodic déjà vu experiences. In primitive societies, so the animists argued, these kinds of events generated beliefs in the existence of other realms with other beings. Accepting this premise, primitive man could then conclude that a spirit being lived in him, was released during sleep (and thus appeared in dreams), and permanently escaped from its host's body at time of death. These escaped spirits were especially important because they not only were freer to move about but also "represented" their dead hosts. The spirits of departed chiefs, fathers, mothers-in-law, and so forth thus had to be placated. Rituals for the dead, beliefs about afterlife, and pantheons became natural extensions of the premise regarding spirit beings. Religion, thus, was seen as an irrational response to a rational quest for explanation.

Animism is no longer considered a true explanation of religion. Tylor, with whom the animism theory is chiefly associated, presented the details of this theory in 1871,[1] and the prevailing question in his work was that of the *origin* of religion. Questions incorrectly asked seldom yield answers correctly understood, and Tylor's was no exception; for, as we shall argue toward the end of this chapter, though his answer has great relevance for the sociology of religion, it

---

[1] E. B. Tylor, *Primitive Culture*, 2 vols. (New York: Harper & Row, 1958). Volume II contains the discussion of animism.

has little to do with the question of origins. Neanderthal and Cro-Magnon men apparently had religion. At least, archaeological evidence suggests that they took special pains with burial, had "sacred" places, and called upon special powers to help in hunts. But the *beginnings* of beliefs and practices taking place as recently as 50,000 or 100,000 years ago, even when they exist in modified form today, are unlikely ever to be known. As William J. Goode has stated, conjectures about "how, under what conditions, man began to believe in divine beings nearly a million years ago must remain sheer speculation."[2] The fault with animism lay not in its answer but in its question. The ultrarationalism of Tylor's day was too much reflected in his approach to religion.

Before we specify how this ultrarationalism stood in the way of the primitive materials tradition, let us look at another example: naturism. F. Max Müller, this school's foremost spokesman,[3] followed Tylor's strategy in that he, too, was seeking the origin of religion. The key, Müller asserted, was to be found in such natural events as storms, sunrises, tides, and other awe-inspiring physical acts of nature. Primitive man, fearful and at the mercy of these events, created beliefs wherein divine agents controlled natural forces. In an ingenious step within ultrarationalism Müller connected the event with the agent by noting an artifact of language. Man has difficulty conceiving and speaking in action terms without suggesting the presence of agents. If one man can toss another around, then when a man is being tossed around in his boat, some agent must be

---

[2] William J. Goode, *Religion Among the Primitives* (New York: Free Press, 1951), p. 22.

[3] F. Max Müller, *Lectures on the Origin and Growth of Religion* (London: Longmans, 1878).

doing the tossing. If one can recognize another pouring water on him, then getting wet in the rain suggests that something pours that water, too. From the notion of agents controlling natural events, the distance is short to notions of gods, their purposes, and their desires. Primitive man went that distance, said the naturists, and that is the way religion began.

Being contemporaries, Tylor and Müller were vulnerable to many of the same intellectual distortions. One of these distortions, as we already remarked, was evolutionism—in their case, the notion that present-day religion is a natural outgrowth of prior stages and that "primitive" religion, if its origins could be explained, would provide a theory of all religion. Neither the animists nor the naturists, however, were as naïve as we have portrayed them; they did not really believe that they were explaining "all" of religion, for example, nor did Tylor discount entirely the influence of natural events or Müller the influence of man's "experiencing" himself in dreams. Where the evolutionary root idea stood most in their way was in the twin assumptions of linearity and ultrarationality. If one were to understand present-day religion, they assumed, he should study first the religions of primitives; and if one seeks the source of primitive religion, he should look at the *content* of beliefs and practices, because they are rationally connected to their source.

The danger involved in these assumptions can be acute. A society, primitive or otherwise, may, for instance, depend heavily upon the sea for its subsistence. It might be entirely understandable, therefore, if the deities of that society were thought to live in the sea and if they were thought to control tides, influence ocean storms, oversee the safety of boats, determine the supply of fish, and so forth. But the sea itself could hardly be considered the *origin* of religion because so many societies *not* dependent upon the sea also have religions. The nature or shape or content of religious beliefs and practices, in other words, may be accounted for by social factors having little or nothing to do with the reason why people are led to have religious sentiments in the first place. The latter, which might be considered the question of man's capacity or inclination for religion, must be kept separate from the question of the form a religion takes. That primitive man dreamed and saw himself in pools of water, in other words, may help to explain why, when confronted with the "need" for religion, he selected those experiences as models for his religious sentiments; but the fact that he had those experiences does not necessarily explain his "need" for religion.

These two questions—why man has the capacity for religious sentiments and why religious sentiments take the form they do—were not kept separate in the primitive materials tradition because of twin errors: primitive man was credited with too much rationality in his religious impulses, and modern religion was seen as an inevitable development of those same impulses. One more illustration of the confusion between capacity and form, though for somewhat different reasons, can be seen in Sigmund Freud's early theory of religion, another in the primitive materials tradition.[4]

Primitive Religion and Universal Neurosis

Freud's interest in religion as an object of study came from the similarities between the neurotic behavior he observed in his patients and the religious behavior he

---

[4] Sigmund Freud, *Totem and Taboo*, trans. A. A. Brill (New York: Vintage, 1960).

read about among Australian primitives. Noting that both
the compulsive neurotic's reaction to the feared object and
the primitive's reaction to his totemic symbol could be characterized as "holy dread," Freud reasoned that the explanation of neuroses might explain the origins of religion. Much
of psychoanalytic theory had been built around instances of
phobias or compulsive behavior, and it explained these
aberrations as resulting from an ambivalence felt toward
the father. The father, hated and loved, feared and admired, could not be attacked or approached openly, so the
ambivalence was redirected to a substitute—dogs, perhaps,
or rabbits. Similarly, the Australian totem clans reacted to
their totems and totem symbols (the kangaroo, for example,
or the taro plant) with ambivalence. At once sacred and
feared, extraordinary but commonplace, the totem was
treated as qualitatively different from other objects. Moreover, Freud noted, persons of the same clan typically felt
strong bonds with one another and respected the incest
taboo extending to all fellow members.

What could account for this series of practices? In *Totem
and Taboo* (1913), Freud supplied an answer: "The basis
of taboo is forbidden action for which there exists a strong
inclination in the unconscious."[5] The totem, therefore, symbolizes a feared desire; if the strongest taboos are against
killing the totem (or harming its symbol) and having sexual
intercourse with a fellow clan member, then these must be
unconsciously desired. In an allegorical account Freud suggested that early in the history of man, the "father" of the
tribe, keeping all the females to himself, incurred the anger
of his "sons."

> One day the expelled brothers joined forces, slew and ate
> the father, and thus put an end to the father horde. To-

---

[5] *Ibid.*, p. 44.

> *gether they dared and accomplished what would have*
> *remained impossible for them singly. Perhaps some ad-*
> *vance in culture, like the use of a new weapon, had given*
> *them the feeling of superiority. Of course, these cannibal-*
> *istic savages ate their victim. This violent primal father*
> *had surely been the envied and feared model for each of*
> *the brothers. Now they accomplished their identification*
> *with him by devouring him and each acquired a part of*
> *his strength. The totem feast . . . would be the repetition*
> *and commemoration of this memorable, criminal act with*
> *which so many things began, social organization, moral*
> *restrictions, and religion.*[6]

Aware, in other words, that subsequent killings among them could occur and filled with remorse, the brothers "undid their deed by declaring that the killing of the father substitute, the totem, was not allowed, and renounced the fruits of their deed by denying themselves the liberated women. Thus they created two fundamental taboos of totemism . . ."[7] The memory of that first act lives on in the "mass psyche," and the sense of guilt survives. It reaches full elaboration, according to Freud, in the Christian myth wherein reconciliation with the father takes place following the son's sacrifice; communion among the brothers involves now the flesh and blood of the son, not that of the father.

---

6 *Ibid.*, p. 183.

7 *Ibid.*, p. 185. Note that in all this, Freud reflects the tendency both of Judaism generally and of nineteenth-century European social scientists in particular to deprecate and ignore the role of the woman. Freud's explanation is explicitly relevant to men (fathers, sons, brothers, and so forth), but one wonders how he would account for female religiosity—a problem all the more vexing because women are generally more religiously involved than men, at least in the contemporary United States and in Catholic countries. For a discussion of Freud's analysis of religion in the context of his life and work, see Philip Rieff, *Freud: The Mind of the Moralist* (Garden City, N.Y.: Anchor Books, 1961).

Freud went beyond the exaggerated allegory and the postulated mass-psyche link in his subsequent essays on religion. *The Future of an Illusion* (1928) and *Civilization and Its Discontents* (1930), though similar in many ways to *Totem and Taboo,* made at least one crucial modification in his explanation. In these later writings Freud allowed that man is instinctively drawn to more than hatred-love for the father and sexual contact with the mother. Aggressiveness and the libido are *generally* seen as raw drives that culture must control. Moreover, in its effort to solve these "problems," culture creates still others. In short, man is doomed to have some frustrations. Religion is one reaction to frustrated instincts; the gods may control the terrors of nature, reconcile one to the cruelty of fate, and explain the evil in the human community.

It is clear (and, for our purposes, instructive to see) what has happened. Beginning his analysis with examples of primitive tribes, Freud was unwittingly led to seek an explanation for totemism, with its accompanying incest taboo and ambivalence toward the totem. The *content* of the Australians' religion, in other words, dictated how he posed the question of why there was religion in the first place, and the answer supplied in the earlier essay is a mixture of answers to both questions. There, for example, Freud could say that " psychoanalytic investigation of the individual teaches with special emphasis that God is in every case modelled after the father and that our personal relation to God is dependent upon our relation to our physical father, fluctuating and changing with him . . ."[8]

It is now known that the Oedipal situation is not universal and therefore is not instinctive; it depends instead on

---

8 Freud, *op. cit.,* p. 190.

a peculiarly strong relationship with another who is both loved and feared.[9] The father and son bond is such a relationship in much of the Western world, just as Freud found it to be among middle-class Viennese at the turn of the century. Perhaps it also obtained among the tribal peoples in Australia. But in societies where the father and son bond is not particularly ambivalent, religion nevertheless has developed. Therefore, though *which* bonds are peculiarly strong may influence the nature of religious sentiments (for example, whether deities are male or female, benevolent or vindictive), it may be the *presence* of *any* crucial (emotionally laden and frustrating) relationship that brings forth the capacity for religious sentiments. Freud came, more or less, to this point in the later essays. Aggressiveness is endemic to social life, just as the libidinous drive is, and to be kept in check the drives must be frustrated. Freud said, then, that frustration, not the particular relationship or event providing the frustration, is the key to the "origin" of religious sentiment.

Without accepting yet the correctness of this point about frustration as the source of religious sentiments, we can at least recognize the significant shift in the implied question being asked. No longer is it "How did this religion begin, and thus how might all religions have begun?" Instead, two questions arise and get sorted out: "What are the roots of religious sentiments in man?" and "What determines the form such sentiments take?" This healthy development for the sociology of religion had been anticipated several years earlier than Freud's writings by the German sociologist

---

[9] Another figure in the sociology of religion makes his appearance now, Bronislaw Malinowski. He discovered no Oedipus complex (as Freud described) in the matrilineal Trobriand Islands, thus calling into question its universality. See *Sex and Repression in Savage Society* (Cleveland: Meridian Books, 1955). We shall reintroduce Malinowski later in this chapter.

Georg Simmel, who was *not* part of the primitive materials tradition. He wrote:

> *The genetic explanation of religion must not only embrace the historical origin of its tradition, but its present energies also which allow us to acquire what has come down to us from the fathers; so that in this sense there are really "origins" of religion whose appearance and effectiveness be long after the "origin" of religion.*[10]

In Freud's case, the generalized answer to the question of religion's "present energies" lay in the motivating force released when frustration is overcome. With religion, he said, "We are perhaps still defenseless, but no longer helplessly paralyzed."[11]

A remarkably different answer was given by Freud's contemporary Emile Durkheim.[12] Durkheim's major work on religion, *The Elementary Forms of the Religious Life* (1912), had just been published when *Totem and Taboo* was being written. But Freud, though he referred to Durkheim's "erroneous" theory explaining tribal choice of totems, evidenced nothing to suggest that he understood the central thesis Durkheim was propounding, nor did he indicate an awareness that their two approaches might be complementary. As we address this possible complementarity, we shall discover not only more insight from the primitive materials tradition but also another source of confusion in the sociology of religion.

---

10 Georg Simmel, "A Contribution to the Sociology of Religion," trans. W. W. Elwang, *American Journal of Sociology*, 10 (November 1905), 359–376. Reprinted in *American Journal of Sociology*, 60 (May 1955), 1–18.

11 Sigmund Freud, *The Future of an Illusion*, trans. W. D. Robson-Scott (Garden City, N.Y.: Anchor Books, 1964), p. 25.

12 Emile Durkheim, *The Elementary Forms of the Religious Life*, trans. J. W. Swain (New York: Free Press, 1947).

Society as Source and Consequence of Religious Sentiment

℣ Durkheim's intellectual life was devoted to the issues of morality and social cohesion. His first monograph, *The Division of Labor in Society*, had identified the shifting basis of social cohesion as related to the extent of occupational specialization and mutual interdependency in society.[13] Later, however, Durkheim sought to supplement such structural explanations of solidarity by putting more explicit emphasis on moral factors such as religion itself. In keeping with the evolutionism of his day, he too went to primitive peoples in order to understand religion's "elementary" forms. However, unlike his predecessors, Durkheim sought to "find a means of discerning the ever-present causes upon which the most essential forms of religious thought and practice depend."[14] He was seeking, in other words, not the "very first beginning" but the forces that *maintain* religious sentiment. The other issue, he said, "has nothing scientific about it, and should be resolutely discarded."[15]

The major distinguishing characteristic of religion, Durkheim noted, is that it deals with *sacred*, not *profane*, things. Sacred things are "set apart and forbidden," whereas profane objects are ordinary. Moreover, sacredness may be imputed to almost anything; sacred character, that is, resides not in the object but in the mind of the beholder. Such being the case, the reason why any particular object is made sacred may be quite different from the reason why persons

---

[13] For this Durkheimian question asked in a contemporary setting, see Phillip E. Hammond, "Secularization, Incorporation, and Social Relations," *American Journal of Sociology*, 72 (September 1966), 188–194.

[14] Durkheim, *op. cit.*, p. 20.

[15] *Ibid.*

are led to impute sacredness to objects. The separation of the two questions is thus complete, and the Durkheimian theory, as a consequence, takes a radically different direction.

In the case of the central Australian tribe, the sacred sphere is intimately joined with the totem. Specifically, at least four elements of totemism are classed apart: (1) the totemic emblem; (2) the thing (usually an animal or plant) that the emblem symbolizes; (3) the members of the clan possessing the totem; and (4) the ideas or beliefs that, via the totem, explain the cosmos. Animism and naturism accounted for the collective totem by saying it was an extension of individual totems. They theorized that ancestor worship, fear of spirits, or cataclysmic natural events generated in individuals a religious (totemic) response that then spread to the collectivity. Durkheim, however, rejected these explanations[16] and reasoned instead that religious sentiments are generated by social organization, by collective life itself. The totem, that is to say, represents a force found in each individual but not coequal with any one individual, a force that is real (it is universally felt), physical, and morally binding. This force is the force of the clan, and Durkheim's statement led to its now-famous restatement that religion is the worship of society.

It is not strange, Durkheim argued, that people (all people, not just primitives) consider society sacred. Society gives the sensation of perpetuity. It commands respect and issues orders that are obeyed even though rational calculation deems them unwise. Even "irrefutable" science is refuted if it counters public opinion too much. The moral pressure felt by individuals as coming from outside themselves—is not this feeling intensified in groups? Does not

<hr>

[16] See *ibid.*, pp. 194–215.

the speaker to a crowd feel his power increased?[17] This force, this power, is very real. We use language we did not invent and instruments we did not make; we invoke rights and responsibilities we did not ourselves generate. Is it not natural that such a force can inspire sentiments of awe, of majesty, of sacredness? And how better can man conceive of this force than with religious ideas? Religion is, then, "before all . . . a system of ideas with which the individuals represent to themselves the society of which they are members, and the obscure but intimate relations which they have with it."[18]

Observing the demands of faith, therefore, is observing the demands of society. Exercising the bonds of religion is strengthening the bonds of society's hold on individuals. "The believer who has communicated with his god is not merely a man who sees new truths of which the unbeliever is ignorant; he is a man who is stronger."[19] Nor is this belief erroneous: "for it is an eternal truth that outside of us there exists something greater than us, with which we enter into communication."[20]

Durkheim had a great deal more to say—comments about why particular totems are chosen; descriptions of totemistic practices; discussions of piacular, imitative, and commemorative rites; and so on—but for our purposes his insight is already very clear: There is within social life itself the force for generating religious sentiment. Persons are capable of viewing their relationships with others as religiously grounded, as morally binding. Religion, then, is a

---

[17] For a dramatic first-person account, see John Dollard, *Caste and Class in a Southern Town*, 3rd ed. (Garden City, N.Y.: Anchor Books, 1949), pp. 242–244.

[18] Durkheim, *op. cit.*, p. 257.

[19] *Ibid.*, p. 464.

[20] *Ibid.*, p. 257.

societal phenomenon, not reducible to faulty rationality or individual emotional trauma.

We have, now, a series of "explanations" of religion, a quartet of theories that not only provide different answers but also are generated by different questions. These theories begin with animism and naturism, which sought the "origin" of religion, and conclude with the works of Freud and Durkheim, which sought the ever-present features of life capable of producing in man feelings that might be called religious sentiment.

Numerous objections have, of course, been raised against the thesis in *The Elementary Forms of the Religious Life*, ranging from charges of anthropological and historical naïveté to charges of ideological heresy.[21] Let us now examine a few that are especially instructive. One concerns the debate over what George C. Homans calls "the social contract theory versus the social mold theory,"[22] an issue disputed by Bronislaw Malinowski and A. B. Radcliffe-Brown, two other prominent figures in the primitive materials tradition. Here the problem is that of individual versus social causes of religion and, more generally, that of isolating causes and effects. Both matters reverberate throughout social theory, but in the sociology of religion the reverberations are perhaps especially important, in part because Durkheim, one of the original parties to the dispute, has been so influential in this area.

Aristotle, of course, had long ago distinguished the several meanings of the word "cause." Does a hat exist that a

---

21 For a summary of these objections, see Imogen Seger, *Durkheim and His Critics on the Sociology of Religion* (New York: Bureau of Applied Social Research, Monograph series. Columbia University, 1957).

22 George C. Homans, *The Human Group* (New York: Harcourt, Brace & World, 1950), pp. 313–333.

man may be kept dry in the rain or because someone made the hat? Does a person brush his teeth because he was told to or because he will have fewer cavities? When individual behavior alone is considered, such questions are typically resolved by referring to levels of motivation—predispositions, facilities, goals, consequences, and so forth. But when an item of *group,* as well as individual, behavior is considered, the matter is greatly complicated. The group may benefit from the activity of some of its members, but those members may engage in that activity for reasons entirely removed from the group consequence. Now, why does the activity persist?

Durkheim, to this question also, gave a radical answer. Social behavior, he said, has social causes. The ensuing confusion can be detected in his famous definition of religion as "a unified system of beliefs and practices relative to sacred things . . . *which unite into one single moral community* . . . all those who adhere to them."[23] Here he is saying that the *consequence* of religion is a cohesive group and that cohesion is the source of religious sentiments. The individual activity of believing and practicing religion is a response to demands of the group, demands that have a life of their own independent of individuals.

Note that several difficulties are suggested here only to loom larger in the full exposition of his thesis. And actually, Durkheim took this position largely for methodological and chauvinistic reasons. Coming out of the tradition of positivism, he very early championed the "social fact" as the distinctive subject matter of sociology and then held, as a matter of principle, that one social fact could only be caused by another social fact, thus escaping the realm of

---

[23] Durkheim, *op. cit.,* p. 62. (Italics added.)

psychology altogether.[24] Later in *The Elementary Forms of the Religious Life,* he had only to plug in the relevant terms: religion (one social fact) could only be determined by society (another social fact) and certainly not by individual needs. In this connection, Durkheim made an important error of excess. Because of his positivistic commitment to facts as "things," he regarded both social facts and society itself as concrete entities, rather than appreciating their role as forceful abstractions and understanding that illusions frequently wield enormous social power on their own. This treatment of abstractions as things has been called the fallacy of "reification"; but there are two other fallacies also lurking in Durkheim's definition and further treatment of religion: those of *tautology* and *circularity.* The tautology emerges because Durkheim defined religion as "that which unifies" only to "discover" later that religion actually seems to unify—a finding guaranteed by the original definition. Finally, the circularity is related to the cause-and-effect issue. At points Durkheim argued that religion is produced by social cohesion; at other points he argued that social cohesion is a product of religion; and at still other points he had it both ways in the same paragraph and even in the same sentence.

As damaging as these errors are, however, it is important not to regard them as disqualifications of the Durkheimian thesis. They are indeed errors of misplaced zeal, and they stem largely from Durkheim's attempt to take mere proposi-

---

24 For Durkheim's most thorough discussion of these points, see *The Rules of the Sociological Method* (New York: Free Press, 1950). For a classic analysis of the various respects in which Durkheim's aspirations and philosophy get in the way of his sociology, see Talcott Parsons, *The Structure of Social Action* (New York: Free Press, 1949), especially Chapter XI.

tions and cloak them in the guise of irrefutable truth. Thus, if we return to Durkheim's definition of religion above, it is unquestionably wiser to consider it as a proposition. *If* social cohesion may be a consequence of religion, the conditions under which it comes about are important to know. And if cohesion is a problematic consequence, then obviously cohesion is not a *necessary* source of religious sentiments. The range of possible sources is thus opened; and cohesion becomes a possible outcome, along with other possibilities. The anthropologist Robert H. Lowie, in criticizing Durkheim, made the first half of this point in his rhetorical question "In what sense are natural phenomena less real than society?"[25] That is, why cannot fear of the unknown, awe felt at cataclysmic events, dreams, and so on also be considered as potential sources of religion? And the second half of the point lay at the bottom of the quarrel between Malinowski and Radcliffe-Brown, the former arguing that only individual motives can account for individual behavior (the "social contract" theory), the latter (a Durkheim disciple) arguing that individual motives would not exist were it not that society needed and provided for them (the "social mold" theory). Since Homans has so masterfully outlined their positions, we can do no better than to quote him as he discussed the hypothetical case of childbirth:

> *Malinowski would emphasize the anxiety aroused by the approach of childbirth itself, while Radcliffe-Brown emphasizes the anxiety aroused by the rites of childbirth: the fear of what would happen if the rites were not properly performed. And just as Malinowski would say that the function of the rites is to relieve individual anxiety and to give confidence, so Radcliffe-Brown would say that their*

---

[25] Robert H. Lowie, *Primitive Religion* (New York: Boni and Liveright, 1924), p. 162.

*function is to contribute to the survival of the society by
making a solemn occasion of a vitally important activity . . .*[26]

The two positions are reconcilable, as Homans persuasively demonstrated,[27] but only at the cost of foregoing the search for *the* cause of religion, distinguishing instead the question of the capacity for religious sentiments (already separated from the explanation of their content) from the question of religion's consequences. As Homans summarized:

*Although magic [religion] is an expression of the emotions
of individuals in the face of danger and uncertainty, it is
also performed as a matter of obedience to social norms.
Society, demanding the performance of ritual and specifying the dreadful consequences of nonperformance, creates,
in part, the anxiety that magic [religion] alleviates. Magic
[religion], moreover, has a function in helping the group
to survive, both by giving confidence to individuals and by
solemnizing, for the group, activities of essential importance. The social contract theory, which holds that social
behavior results from the characteristics of individuals,
and the social mold theory, which holds that individual
behavior results from the characteristics of society, are
both correct, both incomplete, and complementary to one
another.*[28]

---

[26] Homans, *op. cit.*, pp. 325–326.

[27] *Ibid.*, pp. 326–330.

[28] *Ibid.*, p. 330. The reader will note that Homans uses the word "magic," but we have inserted, as a synonym, "religion." The relationship between the two phenomena has been the subject of much discussion in the primitive materials tradition, though it is not central to our discussion here. The classic statement is Bronislaw Malinowski, "Magic, Science, and Religion," in *Magic, Science, and Religion and Other Essays* (Garden City, N.Y.: Anchor Books, 1955), pp. 17–92. For excellent summaries of the prior and ensuing debate, see Goode, *op. cit.*, pp. 50–55; and Edward Norbeck, *Religion in Primitive Society* (New York: Harper & Row, 1961), Chapters 3–4.

Returning to Durkheim, then, we can see that of signal importance in the primitive materials tradition is his insight that social life itself can generate the sensation of "sacredness," that *another* explanation for man's capacity for religious sentiments is his involvement in moral relationships with others. And the significant way of putting the equation of religion and society, as Talcott Parsons said, is "not 'religion is a social phenomenon' so much as 'society is a religious phenomenon.' "[29] Durkheim's insight arises chiefly from his noting that persons' attitudes of respect toward religious ideas and toward moral rules are identical. But the possible consequences this societal sacredness may have for the cohesion of society must, for Durkheim's insight to have full impact, remain separate. Social cohesion is not an automatic religious outcome; the "social" functions must be distinguished from the "individual" functions.

Even if this approach rescues Durkheim from some of his more philosophical errors, there are still other problems worth mentioning. For example, there is certainly a sense in which Durkheim glossed over some contradicting evidence in order to make his case that religion unifies. Thus, his ethnography indicates that totemism's principal unit is not the whole society but rather particular clans within it. Worship of a sacred object, therefore, has little necessary bearing on larger societal integration, and it even allows for possible friction between clans so that society as a whole may become an arena for the expression of religiously grounded hostility over such matters as marriage, inheritance, and politics.[30]

---

29 Parsons, *op. cit.*, p. 427.

30 Part of the difficulty here relates to Durkheim's philosophical and stylistic bent. He tended to think and argue in terms of dichotomies, but many are "false dichotomies" upon closer inspection.

This reasoning points to a larger problem: neglecting the possible negative "social" functions of religion and hence overlooking religion as a source of societal conflict and change. Durkheim is often accused of making little provision for social change. Because religion is seen as the core of society and as intrinsically conservative, change might seem actually to be disallowed! Here is a major difference between the perspectives of Durkheim and Max Weber, the theorist to occupy us in the next chapter. Weber saw religion as one *source* of societal change, but he was not part of the primitive materials tradition and was analyzing religion against the historical development of a complex society. As we shall see later (Chapter VI), modern society often contains friction between religious and other groups seeking to integrate the society; it is this friction that Durkheim leaves unacknowledged.

This tendency is certainly evident in his major distinction between "society" and the "individual," for the clan is only one of a myriad of groups that are interposed between the two poles and offer alternatives of theoretical explanation. A similar point can be made concerning several other dichotomies crucial to Durkheim's architectonic thesis. First, he makes a good deal of the distinction between the "sacred" or important and the "nonsacred" or unimportant in society, but he tends to ignore those facets of social life that are secular but also very important. Thus, anything that is important is, by definition, sacred for Durkheim. Certainly the full recognition of the secular would limit the relevance of religion to society; indeed, this may have been one reason why Durkheim was reluctant to make such recognition formally. Or consider the important distinction between "beliefs" and "rites" as the two aspects of religion itself, subsuming all others. As we shall see, much of the subsequent work in the sociology of religion has sought to elaborate the different aspects of religion in order to give other dimensions such as ethics, ideology, organization, and personal experiences more attention. This approach too provides a richer, more realistic but more problematic view of the components and their interrelations. Once again, Durkheim may have resisted it for precisely this reason.

Sophisticated Issues and Primitive Materials

We have scanned several theories or "answers" from the primitive materials tradition of religion. As answers, much of this early work must be rejected because the questions to which they are responses were inadequately framed. When juxtaposed with different questions, however, we find a rich variety of insights. We conclude this discussion, therefore, with a brief review of these insights set in the context of the contemporary sociological analysis of religion.

First, it is quite clear that the origin, in the sense of very first beginnings, of religion cannot be known in any scientific way. But in the sense that primitive man, like contemporary man, experienced wrenching and overwhelming events, we can surmise for him (as we introspect and confirm in conversation with others) a number of features built into the very quality of life itself—features capable of producing what might be called religious sentiments. From Tylor, Müller, and others we can recognize that mysterious phenomena like dreams, natural cataclysms, or death might well qualify as such features. From Freud and others we are also alerted to the strategic importance that social relationships laden with power and love can have; hence, peculiarly volatile relationships, capable of intense rewards as well as punishments, constitute another of these features. The unpredictability of disaster and the less horrendous problem of the unpredictability of good fortune are variations on the same theme: to live with any zest at all is to be vulnerable, and human vulnerability is one of the features productive of religious sentiments.

Durkheim expands the theme even more. All social relationships have a moral component—an element left unquestioned[31]—and man's response inevitably includes, therefore, some of the "sacred" character more easily recognized in nominally religious behavior. Interaction on any basis other than brute force involves some trust. And what is trust but the recognition of moral obligation?

Now, of course, the saliency of these features can change. We can *probably* assume that dreams were more mysterious to primitives, who understood little of the physiology of sleep, and the study of personality has taken some of the awesomeness out of volatile relationships. But with the increase in empirical understanding has come also an increase in nonempirical implications; it would be foolish to imagine that modern man's knowledge relative to what he would know is greater than primitive man's. The *features* of life productive of religious sentiments, then, though changing in saliency, remain.

More than this can be said. These constant features are of two kinds. Some, which present man with puzzles to be answered, will evoke religious sentiments that are largely cognitive in nature. Nonempirical, these sentiments are tantamount to what generally are called religious beliefs. Propositions that there is a God or there is no God, theologies accounting for the deity's location, relations with the world and men in it, and doctrines regarding proper ritual, the effects of prayer, or disposition of souls—all these and more are essentially cognitive sentiments. They provide answers to empirically unknowable questions. Whatever, in a given society, produces such questions is capable of producing this kind of religious sentiment.

The other kind of religious sentiment is evoked by other features—features presenting man not with puzzles to be

---

31 In *The Division of Labor*, trans. George Simpson (New York: Free Press, 1947), Durkheim refers to "the noncontractual element of contract."

answered but with actions to be evaluated. These latter religious sentiments are largely ethical in nature. Also nonempirical, they are tantamount to morality, the ranking of activities according to their goodness or badness. Freud and especially Durkheim must be credited with the explication here, for they saw how social life compelled men to regard behavior in a moral key. And unless men take life's rewards and punishments as purely random and fortuitous, they arrive at a moral hierarchy. Whatever, in a given society, exposes the moral dimension is capable of producing this second kind of religious sentiment.

The first lesson we can learn from the primitive materials tradition, therefore, is to ask the proper question of its various answers: not "What is the origin of religion?" but "What is it about man that he has everywhere had a religion?" One must, of course, be wary of defining religion too narrowly. To say that unpredictable fate, explosive and emotional relationships, and the moral nexus of social life itself all conspire to generate a capacity for religious sentiment is not necessarily to assert that such sentiment will always follow orthodox lines or result in a church as we normally understand the term. Certainly traditional, otherworldly religion is not the only type of answer or sentiment that may be relevant. One can imagine a society in which other institutions and other ideologies take on religious functions, leaving the church in their wake. Indeed, this was one of the hallmarks of the evolutionary approach. Tylor and Müller certainly envisaged an intellectual transcendence of conventional religion as the unknown became knowable in the evolutionary sequence. Freud looked to psychoanalysis and a scientific morality to liberate man from his religious chains and provide a less arbitrary morality. Even Durkheim held a similar view, hoping to ground societal sentiment in a more meaningful secular philosophy in the West. Durkheim's case is particularly instructive, and it is worth quoting a passage concerning Western religion that appears toward the end of *The Elementary Forms:*

> *If we find a little difficulty today in imagining what* [the] *feasts and ceremonies of the future could consist in, it is because we are going through a stage of transition and moral mediocrity. The great things of the past which filled our fathers with enthusiasm* [Durkheim's father was an orthodox Jewish rabbi though Durkheim himself was a secular freethinker] *do not excite the same ardor in us, either because they have come into common usage to such an extent that we are unconscious of them or else because they no longer answer to our actual aspirations; but as yet there is nothing to replace them. We can no longer impassionate ourselves for the principles . . . of . . . Christianity. In a word, the old gods are growing old or already dead, and others are not yet born. . . . it is life itself, and not a dead past, which can produce a living cult.*[32]

In all this, it is ironic that Tylor, Müller, Freud, and Durkheim should be seen as offering ultimate justifications for religion when they themselves prophesied the eclipse of conventional religion. But this irony illustrates the importance of separating the first legitimate question of man's general religious capacity from a second legitimate question of the form and content of his religion. Let us return to that second question now.

Early anthropologists were divided on whether or not monotheism preceded or followed polytheism and whether or not both would develop into areligion. Better than asking those questions, however, is seeking to account for the form or content—whatever it may be—of any religion. Why are gods conceived as loving by some, as vengeful by others? When are gods coequals in the pantheon, and when ar-

---

[32] Durkheim, *Elementary Forms, op. cit.,* p. 427.

ranged in a hierarchy? Why should some societies extend the prohibition on killing to lower animals or human outsiders, whereas others regard as holy the lives of relatively few? In fact, relatively little is known about the answers to such questions. Anthropological study has typically been of single societies, rendering comparative study unlikely, and studies of contemporary societies have not generally raised the issue. In 1960, however, Guy E. Swanson produced a study that united contemporary sociological survey techniques and the primitive materials tradition, confronting this issue directly.[33]

Using data for 50 societies representing a scheme of some 47 world geographic regions sampling roughly 3,500 societies that have been estimated to exist in world history, Swanson explored the multiple relationships between aspects of social structure and aspects of religious form. For example, he found a strong correlation between the prevalence of witchcraft and the extent of "unlegitimated or uncontrolled relationships" both within any given society and in a society's relationships with outsiders. Thus, witchcraft can be seen as a form of social control that emerges where social control is lacking because social relationships are noncodified and nonstandardized.

In another of Swanson's many findings, one concerning the presence and absence of monotheism, there is a high correlation (.81) between monotheism and the presence of three or more sovereign groups in a society, where a "sovereign group" is defined as one that "exercises original and independent jurisdiction over some sphere of social life," has regular meetings, has three or more members, is legitimate in the eyes of the members, persists over time, and has

---

[33] Guy E. Swanson, *The Birth of the Gods* (Ann Arbor: University of Michigan Press, 1960).

regular decision-making apparatus.[34] Here it seems that monotheism is a reflection of the social structure insofar as both a monotheistic deity and a structure of sovereign groups connote hierarchic principles of authority.

Although Swanson's entire book is surely worth an independent reading for what it brings to the issues at hand, it inevitably leaves some questions dangling. For example, comparing only the two findings noted above, the first indicates that the religious form is a *compensation* for weaknesses in the social structure, but the second suggests that it is merely a *reflection* of the structure itself. There are a number of hypothetical resolutions of this seeming inconsistency; for instance, it may be that the presence of several sovereign groups causes such a differentiation of societal power that a vacuum results, and a monotheistic deity is needed as a compensatory source of unambiguous authority. The point, however, is not to question Swanson or to offer a pretentious reinterpretation. Rather, it is to indicate that problems arise even in the most sophisticated treatments of the valid issues emerging from the primitive materials tradition.

A third lesson to be learned from the primitive materials tradition lies in asking correctly the question of religion's consequences. Human interaction, if it generates mutual moral feelings, must imply common values for those who are party to the interaction. This was Durkheim's great insight. But the conclusion is by no means automatic that society's cohesiveness depends on religion. The oft-stated proposition that "one of the functions of religion is to integrate, through common values, the members of a society" is therefore misleading. What is at issue are the consequences of religion—for believers and nonbelievers, for individuals

---

[34] *Ibid.,* p. 42.

and collectivities. Again, relatively little is known of these matters, especially in the area of consequences for collectivities.[35] Surely, however, one must beware of *assuming* (1) that religion actually does integrate in the first place and (2) that if it integrates at all, this in turn is a "cause" of religion, because religion can come about for a host of reasons having nothing to do with its ultimate consequences.

Nevertheless, the issue of religious consequences remains central both to the primitive materials tradition and to contemporary sociology of religion. Once again, a recent study links the two. William J. Goode's *Religion Among the Primitives* provides comparative case studies of five preliterate societies, with special emphasis on the interlocking network connecting religion with the spheres of politics, economics, and the family.[36] That religion does have consequences is clear in Goode's analysis, but these consequences are investigated, not assumed.

Summary

℈ We have reviewed in this first chapter several of the early theories of religious behavior, theories based on primitive materials. Tylor, Müller, Freud, and Durkheim must certainly be credited with helping us understand religion from the standpoint of social science, even if we can look back and see that many of the questions they asked were not appropriate to the materials in which they sought answers. Nevertheless, the primitive materials tradition is a rich source of sociological insight, by no means exhausted in the few issues discussed in this chapter. To charge that tradition with ultrarationality and evolutionism and then dis-

---

[35] Later discussion, however, will raise this matter again.
[36] Goode, *op. cit.*

miss it as unworthy of contemporary attention is not only arrogance but also ignorance of all it can teach us.[37] The present chapter can do no more than alert the reader to some of the possibilities. For it turns out that, reformulated, the questions of the early theorists are questions being asked today.

---

[37] Indeed, Robert N. Bellah, "Religious Evolution," *American Sociological Review*, 29 (June 1964), 358–374, returns to a modified evolutionary point of view and does so with remarkable insight and payoff, as we shall see in Chapter III.

II

CONTENDING WITH COMPLEXITY:
Max Weber and Early Christianity

One of the goals of the previous chapter was to salvage as much as possible from the primitive materials tradition for application to more complex societies. Although it was possible to rescue broad questions and answers, the result was hardly a full-fledged sociological framework. This chapter moves further in that direction. Here the context shifts from the relatively simple structure of preliterate societies to an epoch in early Western society that witnessed unusual strains and tensions. In the years surrounding the birth of Christianity, religion was no seamless web. Nor did it realize the dream of wholesale societal integration that so entranced Emile Durkheim and other functionalists.[1] Religion was at best a fragmented institution whose factions competed among themselves but also with nonreligious aspects of the society.

Christianity was a movement that combined cultural strains of East and West and one that arose as an aberrant Jewish response to a cultural crisis. Classical Greek civilization had lost its thrust and moved from the exquisite to the barbarous. Christianity sought a remedy for people in need of one. Even so, it faced an uphill battle. As the distinguished church historian and comparative religionist A. C. Bouquet remarked, ". . . so gross, so petty, even superstitious and wrong-headed were many of the blundering attempts to explain the significance of Jesus for the world, that to the impartial observer the one and only perfectly attested miracle (in the old fashioned sense) must seem the

---

[1] This allusion to the functionalist's dream is an "in" reference that may best be kept in. However, it refers to the tendency of a few social theorists to view even the most complex societies as organic systems that attain stable and lasting equilibria. As the preceding chapter pointed out, Durkheim's analyses of primitive society and its religion have given spurious encouragement to this perspective. Not only is full equilibrium a rare commodity in complex societies but it is even scarce among less differentiated tribes. Not only is religion far from a panacea for disorganization, but it may even provoke disorganization. Still, this is not to impugn all functionalists or to suggest that societal integration always gives way before conflict and divisiveness. Functionalism remains a noble and provocative posture; its foremost proponents take integration as a question rather than an article of faith. Such proponents have advanced sociology considerably beyond its nineteenth-century traces in their advocacy of systematic theory generally. For further exploration of the continuing debate surrounding functionalism (a debate that is central to virtually all the recent developments in sociological theory), see the recent reader edited by N. J. Demerath III and Richard A. Peterson, *System, Change and Conflict* (New York: Free Press, 1967).

fact of the vital and active existence of the Christian movement in the world today."[2]

Now it is confessedly intimidating for a sociologist to
confront the scholarship surrounding the "early church."
Few lodes have been mined so heavily or so painstakingly
by so many experts. Few topics excite more vested interests.
Let it be clear that what follows is not meant to be a substitute for the historical research that has gone before or an
effort to summarize it fully. Ours is cursory history at best.
It is history not for its own sake, but rather as a means of
introducing some important sociological concepts in a manner that is not so abstract as to alienate.

The concepts that follow share a common source in the
one man who eclipses Durkheim as a forefather of the
current sociology of religion. Max Weber is most widely
known for a volume to be considered in the next chapter,
The Protestant Ethic and the Spirit of Capitalism,[3] but
many consider this his poorest work in spite of its renown.
Certainly Weber's contributions to religion range far beyond the Protestant Reformation; they extend to trenchant
analyses of Confucianism, Hinduism, ancient Judaism, and
early Christianity as well. All this and more is manifest in

---

[2] A. C. Bouquet, *Comparative Religion* (Baltimore: Penguin, 1941),
p. 243. Although a great deal has been and will be said concerning
Christianity's debt to Judaism, sociologists of religion have paid
relatively little attention to the influence of the Greeks and Romans.
Bouquet offers one of several treatments of the relationship. See
also the monumental though anti-Semitic work of Edward Gibbon,
The Decline and Fall of the Roman Empire, and the brilliant, lively
classic by Gilbert Murray, *Five Stages of Greek Religion* (Garden
City, N.Y.: Anchor Books, 1955).

[3] Max Weber, *The Protestant Ethic and the Spirit of Capitalism,*
trans. Talcott Parsons (New York: Scribner, 1928; paperback ed.
1958).

his recently translated classic *The Sociology of Religion*[4]—
the book upon which this chapter leans most heavily.

Before we turn to Weber's analysis of religion, let us
briefly consider his general analytical style. Although much
of Weber's work is cast in an awesome morass of historical
detail, he was most stimulating in his use of the "ideal
type," a methodological strategy of distorting reality to en-
hance our appreciation of it. For example, Weber's famous
ideal type of "bureaucracy" was self-consciously unrealistic;
he was at pains to indicate that no existing bureaucratic
arrangement would fulfill the concept perfectly. The model
was instead designed as a benchmark against which reality
might be assessed: How do existing bureaucracies depart
from the ideal characterization, why, in what direction, and

---

[4] Max Weber, *The Sociology of Religion*, trans. Ephraim Fischoff
(Boston: Beacon Press, 1963). This was one of Weber's last works
and perhaps a bit of Weber's chronology is in order here. His work
on religion began essentially with his initial study of Protestantism
and the rise of capitalism, a monograph first published in 1905.
Until 1910, he was engaged in a steady stream of exchanges concerning the work, and in 1911 he launched a series of comparative
analyses of the religions of China and India and ancient Judaism.
Here the object was to pick societies in which there were funda-
mentally the same preconditions for capitalism except one: a suit-
able religious theology. In 1915 or thereabouts, Weber began to
grow more abstract and more systematic in seeking to understand
religion generally. This was part of a larger analysis of social and
economic organization. The resulting unfinished essay was part of a
larger, multivolume work: the famous *Wirtschaft und Gesellschaft*,
truncated by Weber's death in 1920. It is these last essays that are
translated and compiled in *The Sociology of Religion*, essays written
some ten years after the heralded *Protestant Ethic and the Spirit of
Capitalism*. Later we shall suggest some important differences that
occur in Weber's thought over the ten years. Here it suffices to say
that the earlier work is an arresting monograph and the later
product is a monument yet to be eclipsed. But a final word concerning citations. If we were to follow anything like the proper scholarly
procedures in what follows, each page would be riddled with foot-
notes. Weber was not a man to compartmentalize his thoughts; his

to what extent? Note, however, that Weber does not use the term "ideal" to suggest his own personal preference or any normative statement. Instead, it is meant to suggest only that the type is logically deduced from "ideas" rather than empirically induced from reality itself.

Weber's sociology of religion is a confection of such ideal types. Moreover, he had a way of contriving contrasting types so that, like Durkheim, he suspended religion within a web of procrustian dichotomies and trichotomies. Any religious movement could be examined according to its theological proclivities (otherworldly versus this-worldly, mystical versus ascetic); its prophetic beginnings (exemplary versus ethical); its relation to the class structure (whether the child of a dominant status group, the middle classes, the peasantry, or the urban lower classes); its source of authority (charismatic, traditional, or rational-legal); or its structural form (church versus sect). Each of these frameworks produces a theoretical logic of its own. Although none of them fits perfectly the case of developing Christianity, all are relevant either as approximations to the facts or as sharp and guiding contrasts. This chapter does not exhaust the relevant ideal types and abstractions in Weber. In sampling only a few of the most important, it seeks to convey the general approach at the expense of many of its details.

Because of Weber's commanding theoretical interests, he never provided a full-scale chronological history of the rise of Christianity, but left the task to his student and colleague Ernst Troeltsch.[5] Weber was content to weave bits of the

<hr>

several ideas on a single subject range throughout his prolific publications. For this reason, and because this book is meant more as a tantalizer than a tome, we shall restrict ourselves to citations of major ideas and their major treatments. In addition, we shall provide later references to a number of trots and secondary sources for those who wish to pursue the matter further.

[5] Ernst Troeltsch, *The Social Teaching of the Christian Churches*, 2 vols., trans. Olive Wyon (New York: Macmillan, 1932).

chronology into his various theoretical discussions—the tack we shall follow as well. This chapter is organized not in terms of dates and periods but rather in terms of concepts. Each provides a new perspective with which to illumine a different facet of the early church and its development. Moreover, and more important, each has continuing relevance for the contemporary scene.

Otherworldly Asceticism as a Theological Perspective

Perhaps Weber's most profound contribution to the development of sociology in general was to restore the importance of ideas and cultural factors after their Marxian, materialistic purge.[6] Weber argued that values have an influence that is not always reducible to matters of social class or societal structure; he asserted that noneconomic aspects of life are vital, independent forces in their own right. All these assertions can be seen most clearly in his focus on theology[7] and, of course, make up the central

---

6 For a general appreciation of Weber the man and his intellectual context see Talcott Parsons, *The Structure of Social Action* (New York: Free Press, 1949), especially pp. 473–694; Reinhard Bendix, *Max Weber: An Intellectual Portrait* (Garden City, N.Y.: Doubleday, 1960); H. Stuart Hughes, *Consciousness and Society* (New York: Random House, 1958); Robert A. Nisbet, *The Sociological Tradition* (New York: Basic Books, 1967); and the assorted introductions to Weber's various translated works by Parsons, Hans Gerth, and C. Wright Mills.

7 For a general statement of Weber's theological analysis, see *The Sociology of Religion, op. cit.*, pp. 166–183, 262–274. Each of the cells in the fourfold table to follow is treated in detail in separate volumes. Thus, for Confucianism, see Weber, *The Religion of China* (New York: Free Press, 1951); for Hinduism, *The Religion of India* (New York: Free Press, 1958); for Judaism, *Ancient Judaism* (New York: Free Press, 1952); and for Catholicism, *The Protestant Ethic and the Spirit of Capitalism, op. cit.* Actually, the book on China covers Taoism as well as Confucianism, and the study of India encompasses Buddhism as well as Hinduism. For an important secondary source on Weber's comparative studies of religion, see Bendix, *op. cit.*, pp. 117–264.

theme of *The Protestant Ethic and the Spirit of Capitalism,* to be considered later. They are equally important in understanding Weber's approach to early Christianity. The crucial question for Weber was always a comparative one. Here the issue concerns Christianity's theological distinctiveness when it is compared with the world's other "great religions."

Weber plumbs the issue with the help of two key dimensions or dichotomies, one concerning the *goals* of the religious life and the other involving the *means* toward these goals. First, he argues that the goals of religion can be either "this-worldly" or "otherworldly." That is, its ultimate rewards and punishments may be rooted either in this life or in the life still to come—Heaven, Hell, Nirvana, and so forth. His second dimension is theoretically independent, which is to say that it may coexist with either an "otherworldly" or a "this-worldly" end and provide the means to both. Here the reference is to the nature of religious action. Some theologies lean toward the "mystical" in that the individual is encouraged to withdraw from worldly action altogether to ponder transcending issues or verities. Other theologies are "ascetic" in their emphasis on "doing" rather than "feeling," their emphasis on religiously motivated behavior within the worldly rounds themselves.

With some oversimplification, much of Weber's analysis is summarized in fourfold Figure 1. The figure is defined by the two dichotomies at issue, one across the top and the other down the side. Each cell refers to a particular combination and to a unique theological syndrome. Thus, the upper–left-hand cell reveals Confucianism as a this-worldly, mystical religion, one that enjoins contemplation of the present life in order to adjust to its rewards and avoid its foibles. Here is an inward effort to make peace with one's environment without altering it. The objective is to har-

	This-Worldly	**Otherworldly**
Mysticism	Confucianism	Hinduism
Asceticism	Judaism	Catholicism

Figure 1. Weber's dichotomies concerning the goals of religious life and the means to these goals.

monize rather than to seek active changes in the name of religion. The upper–right-hand cell offers Hinduism as a second distinctive case. Hinduism, of course, puts great emphasis on reincarnation and on one's fate in future generations within its elaborate caste system. The ultimate objective is to escape the cycle altogether, and mystical contemplation and steadfast endurance are means to these otherworldly ends. There is no premium on either changing present conditions or fully harmonizing with them; present conditions are epiphenomenal to the larger meaning of a life beyond life itself.

Moving from top to bottom and from Eastern to Western religion in the figure, Judaism represents an early approximation of the later qualities of Protestantism. Weber makes a great deal of Judaism's break with Eastern religion as a precursor for subsequent religious development in the West. The Jews joined in a covenant with Jahweh, a covenant that involved ethical duties on behalf of the world and ritual observance on behalf of the individual. Emphasis was on action rather than on contemplation, and the ultimate rewards were to occur as part of this life, whether through the vengeance of a wrathful God or through the coming of a Messiah and the full flowering of the millennium. Here was the beginning of the Western religious

activism that was to find its culmination in Puritanism. The
Jewish covenant with God was an almost rational religious
contract that presaged the Puritan notion of earning one's
salvation.

To some extent, the last cell of the table, on the lower
right, represents a return to the Eastern religious tradition,
a mutation in Western religious development. The early
Christian and Catholic emphasis on otherworldly affairs
marks a change away from Judaism's stress on affairs of this
life and back to the more disembodied plane of Hinduism.
Nor is this a surprise when one considers that Jesus himself
was raised on the Asian side of the Aegean and spoke a
middle-Asian language, with all its attendant images. Certainly the emphasis on both an afterlife and Jesus' own
resurrection are well grounded in Hinduism. Note, however, that Catholicism was not, in Weber's view, a mystical
religion. Being more ascetic, it retained the characteristic
Western stamp of working within the world for changes in
the name of religion itself. This aspect was to be crucial in
its subsequent development.

Theology as an Independent Influence

Because both Confucianism and Hinduism are basi-
cally mystical, their emphasis is on individual contemplation as opposed to social action. Thus, the concept of
religious organization itself is relatively unimportant. The
notion of a church or any instrumentally efficient laity is
virtually alien to the two religious traditions. Not so in the
West. Both Judaism and Catholicism (together with another Jewish offshoot, Islam) have highly developed organizational forms as a way of fulfilling the mandate for aggressively ascetic action in the interests of large-scale social
change. It is true that, for a time, repressive political

measures and geographical dispersion forced Judaism to deemphasize the temple and treat the family as the basic religious unit. Still, Judaism both originated and has maintained the Western view of religious organization as a crucial means to sacred ends.

Theological consequences are also important, however, in distinguishing the *type* of organization that characterized the Jews and the early Christians. Judaism's this-worldly asceticism led to a high degree of political aggressiveness. Its doctrine of "the chosen people" led to a fervent nationalism and a tendency to restrict membership as a form of self-fulfilling prophecy; that is, we are the few partly because we choose to restrict ourselves in number. On the other hand, the early Christians were more universalistic in their otherworldly emphasis. Because their mandate led them to save the world by evangelizing it instead of changing it by defeating it, they were both less exclusive in their recruitment and less aggressive in their political expressions.[8] Here were proselytizers who, unlike the Jews, accepted both women and Gentiles. Because the early Christians were less of a political or nationalistic threat, they were better able to curb the wrath of later Roman authorities and even to win the ultimate support of the emperor Constantine in the famous Edict of Milan (A.D. 313).

But the link between theology and religious organization is not a simple one for Weber. There are important contingencies, one of which concerns the innovator who launches the religious movement in the first place. Weber distin-

---

[8] It would be a mistake to view the early Christians as wholly docile. As Martin Luther King, Jr., was wont to point out, here was an early example of strident civil disobedience in response to Roman persecution. Indeed, some of that persecution was actually courted. For a good brief account of the changing relations between the Christians and the Roman authorities, see R. H. Barrow, *The Romans* (London: Pelican Books, 1949), especially pp. 179–192.

guishes between two ideal-typical sorts of prophets. First, the *exemplary* prophet is more Eastern and best approximated by Confucius and Gautama of the Buddhists. Exemplary leaders are mystics with two implications: (1) they tend to stress a contemplative withdrawal from the affairs of the world, and (2) they provide an individual example but have no aspirations for founding a large-scale organization and serving as its leader. In contrast, the *ethical* or *emissary* prophet is more Western in character and is best represented by the Old Testament Jewish prophets and by Muhammed. These men were activists by impulse; their penchant for social change dictated the need for organization; they were more concerned with assembling troops than waiting for emulators. Whereas the exemplary prophet radiates a sense of inward peace and successful release, the ethical prophet is more politically oriented and communicates restlessness rather than bliss, a drive for change rather than a need to escape or adjust.[9]

Clearly the type of prophet is related to the theological tradition, but the relationship need not be perfect. Although a theology of otherworldly mysticism is unlikely to spawn

---

[9] Weber, *The Sociology of Religion, op. cit.,* pp. 46–79. Note, however, that these pages are concerned with more than the current distinction at issue. In addition to delineating types of prophets, Weber went on to separate the prophet in general from several other types of religious leaders, including the magician, the mystagogue, and the priest. The distinction between the prophet and the priest turns on the difference between the religious entrepreneur and the church official. Weber relied heavily on nineteenth-century German scholarship to document friction between the two categories in the Judaic context, but recent research suggests that the friction was nowhere near as great as once supposed. Thus, ideal-typical contrasts once again live up to their promise of distorting reality. For a fuller discussion of this point and its implications, see Peter L. Berger, "Charisma and Religious Innovation: The Social Location of Israelite Prophecy," *American Sociological Review,* 28 (December 1963), 940–950.

an ethical prophet, such a prophet may occur as a break-through in the established order, producing religious change as a precursor to social change. Although a tradition of this-worldly asceticism is generally inhospitable to an exemplary prophet, Jesus was suspect among the Jews precisely because he departed from the tradition in such a direction. His prophecy was essentially apolitical, and his universalism was a threat to the nationalistic ambitions of the Jews themselves. Here was the kind of breakthrough mentioned above. But rather than treat it as a historical quirk, let us go on to explore more of Weber's theory to gain greater leverage upon the event.

Social Class and the Formation of Religious Movements

We have mentioned that Weber assigned an inde-pendent influence to theology, but it would be a mistake to assume that he regarded theology as *sui generis* or as a spontaneously emergent religious property. The-ology does not spring from the foreheads of the gods but more likely from the social origins of its founding adher-ents. A central theme for both Weber the sociologist and Weber the man was the problem of giving enriched and sustained meaning to the individual in society. The business of culture and especially its religious agent is to justify man's present status and to reconcile his image of "what is" with his vision of "what ought to be." Here is the difficulty of balancing hard work and low achievement, of explaining the unexplainable disaster, of grappling with the antimonies of good and evil as these are manifest in society. Weber used the term "theodicy" to refer to the aspect of doctrine that is devoted to such issues.

Weber approached "theodicy" from two quite different

perspectives.[10] First, he made judgments on the logical elegance and systematic virtues of various theodicies, and he determined that only three measured up fully: Zoroastrian dualism, the Hindu doctrine of reincarnation, and the Calvinist notion of predestination—something to be considered at greater length in the next chapter. Second, however, Weber appraised theodicies for their social functions. Here he asked what type of theodicy is most appropriate for various social classes, and three types can be singled out for special attention. What could be called a theodicy of *dominance* is most appropriate for the elite, for example, warriors, priests, and political leaders. Hinduism provides an example because it arose in large part as the Brahmins' own justification for occupying power and because, in Weber's view, the caste system was largely contrived by those at the top to ensure their power. Clearly, however, a theodicy of dominance is not apt for those who lack dominance itself. With regard to the middle classes (or what Weber terms the civic strata) a theodicy of *mobility* is more to the point. Here there is a premium on economic gain and hence on rationality as a break with the past and a means to personal betterment. (Later, we shall discuss the rise of the Protestant Ethic as a celebrated example.[11]) But just as a

---

[10] Weber, *The Sociology of Religion, op. cit.*, pp. 138–150, 184–222. For a somewhat earlier but no less valuable essay on theodicy and social class, see Hans H. Gerth and C. Wright Mills (eds.), *From Max Weber: Essays in Sociology* (New York: Oxford University Press, 1946), pp. 267–362.

[11] We mentioned earlier that the ten years that elapsed between *The Protestant Ethic and the Spirit of Capitalism* and *The Sociology of Religion* produced a number of significant shifts in Weber's thinking. This change is nowhere more evident than in his discussion of social class and theodicy. As we shall see in the next chapter, the drift of his earlier work suggested that religious doctrine arises somewhat independently of the needs of adherents—a counter to the Marxian position, in which all ideas are merely reflections of the economic order and the thinker's place in that order. Later,

motif of dominance is inappropriate for those who are still undergoing mobility, so is a theme of mobility inappropriate for those who are hopelessly mired among the dispossessed and the disestablished. A theodicy of *escape* is more pertinent to the plight of urban lower classes, the peasantry, and pariah groups. At times the escape may take this-worldly forms through radical social change and political aggressiveness (for example, Judaism); most commonly, however, the escape is otherworldly wherein the adherent receives his deserved riches in a life after death. This, of course, is the theodicy that best approximates the early Christian case.

The rise of Christianity has long been a pawn in the dispute between the Marxists and their opponents. The former hold that it was essentially a proletarian movement and a precursor of more fundamental economic revolts to emerge later. Karl Marx and Friedrich Engels themselves suggested this, and the suggestion was elaborated at length by Karl Kautsky.[12] On the other hand, the thesis has its opponents in the Weberian tradition. Both Weber and his protégé Ernst Troeltsch disputed Christianity's proletarian origins. Weber argued that it was more of a lower middle-class movement; Troeltsch held that it was characterized by

---

however, Weber moved in a more Marxian direction so that doctrine is indeed more reflective of the different needs of social classes, suggesting that the Protestant Ethic arose more in response to the middle class than as a prerequisite for middle-class emergence. Still, Weber has continually suffered from capsule summaries of just this sort. Neither his earlier nor his later work is quite this simple; in fact, he manages to cover himself at various points so as to frustrate any easy summary and challenge any quick assertions of contradiction or change.

[12] See, for example, Friedrich Engels, "On the History of Early Christianity," in Lewis S. Feuer (ed.), *Marx and Engels: Basic Writings on Politics and Philosophy* (Garden City, N.Y.: Anchor Books, 1959), pp. 168–194; Karl Kautsky, *Foundation of Christianity* (New York: A. S. Russell, 1954).

a great deal of status heterogeneity.[13] Certainly there is evidence that it is incorrect to label Jesus the son of a lower-class carpenter. Joseph was, more accurately, a contractor and a skilled craftsman; he was also a distant relative of the local royal family. Note, however, that this itself is hardly sufficient rebuttal to the Marxian position. Marx's portrait of the proletarian revolutionary movement stressed the role of skilled workers as opposed to the totally downtrodden "lumpen proletariat"; the model also featured defecting members of the bourgeoisie, men who would supply brain-power and leadership ability. Thus, data that would seem to rebut the Marxian position are no rebuttal at all when that position is correctly understood; indeed, they help to cement the Marxian case itself.

Still, the early Christians did depart in another crucial respect from the Marxian model. Marx had confidence only in the revolutionary potential of the urban proletariat and was expressly pessimistic about the peasantry's chances of igniting a spark. The rural and small-town folk were no less oppressed, but they were far more dispersed with conse-quent communication problems for developing the requisite "class consciousness." Yet Christianity was, in its begin-nings, a small-town movement. Weber argued at some

---

[13] Troeltsch, op. cit., I, 39–51. Like the early Weber, Troeltsch sought to steer away from the Marxian materialistic conception of religion. Indeed, Troeltsch may have gone too far. He steadfastly insisted that Christianity was "sociologically autonomous" and had ' no characteristics in common with general social movements. He went to great pains to attend to theological delicacies, at the frequent expense of theoretical necessities. Still, Troeltsch did not fall into the void of his predecessors who sought to analyze religion wholly on its own terms. Troeltsch realized the dangers here, and even his own tendencies in this direction were often overridden when push came to shove and the data were in. Certainly his classic delinea-tion of the church-sect distinction is sociology of the first rank, as we shall see later.

length that important religious innovations seldom occur in
great cultural centers. They are more likely to develop in
the provinces, where man is left to contend with his fate in
relative isolation and without the stultifying force of pre-
existing ideologies. Perhaps this reasoning points out the
difference between an aggressive force for *social* revolution
and a less politicized movement for *cultural* change, a
major difference between Judaism and Christianity themselves. Certainly Christianity's small-town base helps to
account for many of its more persistent qualities. Weber
argued that the less urban the context, the weaker the pressures to this-worldly rationality. The Christian emphasis on
miracles and otherworldliness owes much to an inception
that occurred beyond the scope of the worldly constraints
of the urban center. Still, Marx again has a response. Weber
indicated that Christianity began to flourish only after it
was transplanted to an urban setting. Marx's model may be
appropriate to Christianity's later developments if not to its
inception.

Implicit in all this is Weber's theorem that every religious
movement is indelibly stamped with the needs and whims
of its founding status group. It is easy to muster supporting
examples. Hinduism has retained a caste system originated
by the Brahmins from on high. Catholicism has retained a
basic lower-class theodicy of otherworldly escape. There is,
however, room for quibbling, particularly in the Catholic
case. Although it is true that the basic doctrine has remained, it is also true that there have been changes in
ethical and organizational interpretations that reflect new
social class interests. A key aspect of the rise of the Catholic
church and its development from a struggling sect to a
societal-wide institution was a kind of status mobility. What
began as a largely lower-class movement ultimately became

the instrument of the elite after a great deal of pew-fighting and backbiting. As recruitment extended to the Gentiles, as the Roman authorities themselves were evangelized, as the church later became a bastion of medieval feudalism and the lair of lords and princes, Catholicism underwent an agonized but pronounced change. The extent of the change was exemplified by an effort to rewrite church history to provide an aristocratic reinterpretation of Jesus and his apostles as first-century gentlemen of means and honor. The historian G. G. Coulton notes that the medieval lower classes were chided, neglected, and left in the hands of roving monks who were themselves marginal to the church establishment and who avoided identification with church authority while stressing fervent emotionalism rather than the customary rituals.[14] It was not that the peasantry was irreligious; it was just that it became unchurched. Indeed, as Norman Cohn pointed out, the Pope himself was anti-Christ to many.[15]

Nor were the lower classes alone neglected. By the Renaissance, new middle classes were similarly beyond the elitist pale as the church somewhat desperately threw in its lot with the forces of power. (The middle-class reaction will be chronicled later under the discussion of Protestantism.) Meanwhile, this turn suggests two corollaries to Weber's

---

[14] G. G. Coulton, *Medieval Village, Manor, and Monastery* (New York: Harper Torchbooks, 1960), pp. 231–252.

[15] Norman Cohn, *The Pursuit of the Millennium* (New York: Oxford University Press, 1957), p. 21. Cohn's work is a superb study of what may be termed the religious underground. While concentrating on revolutionary religious movements of the dispossessed in medieval Europe, his research extends from pre-Christianity to contemporary totalitarianism. Certainly his concept of "revolutionary eschatology" refers to a distinct and abiding world view that must be confronted in any analysis of lower-class religious movements.

proposition concerning founding status groups. First, religious movements tend to reflect the *ethical and organizational* interests of their highest-ranking substantial status group, even though the founding doctrine and theodicy may remain. Second, the most viable church will maximize status heterogeneity in its members and avoid overidentification with any single social class. Both of these corollaries will be explored at greater length, but here both point to still another conceptual vein in the body of Weberian theory.

Charismatic, Traditional, and Rational-Legal Authority: The Shifting Sands of Legitimation

For all Weber's contributions to religion, religion was not his primary intellectual concern. Personally uncommitted and unaffiliated, Weber studied religion primarily for its relevance to his major theme—changing values and their changing organizational implementations, with special reference to the rise of Western rationality. Indeed, rationality is perhaps the single most revealing clue to Weber's life work. It both appalled and fascinated him, with its mixture of efficiency and relentless secularization. On the one hand, it offered "progress"; on the other, it threatened to rob man of his cultural identity by subjecting all such meaning to clinical and dispassionate analysis. The important point was not that men *were* rational but that they *sought to be*—and with bittersweet consequences. Weber examined this theme not only in religion but also in law, music, architecture, and the rise and refinement of bureaucratic organization and authority.[16] This last focus

---

[16] For several of Weber's publications concerning the rise and consequences of rationality, see Max Rheinstein (ed.), *Max Weber on Law in Economy and Society* (Cambridge, Mass.: Harvard Uni-

overlaps with the others, for issues of authority and organization extend into all substantive fields. It is here that we
glimpse the quintessential Weber—brilliant but ambiguous,
bold yet hesitant.

In dealing with authority, Weber once again asked us to
joust with ideal types. His concern was not so much with
the wielding of authority as with its acceptance and legitimation in the eyes of the followers. Weber proposed three
basic forms of legitimation based on three distinct sorts of
appeals and authentications.[17] First, he stressed the *charismatic* leader as one at the vanguard of wrenching, large-
scale, social changes. Here is a person who combines magic
and creativity, one who not only blazes new paths but is
able to compel others to follow. The charismatic leader
deploys his own exceptional qualities to allay the fears that
accompany change. He exists totally outside of existing
establishments but is able to envelop his followers and
thus provide a nurturance and structure all his own. In
contrast, Weber proposes *traditional* authority as a quite
different type in which the premium is not on change but
rather on conserving the past. The leader's essential legitimacy depends upon his doing what others have done
before him. He is unquestioned because to question him
would be to question generations past. He is recognized not
for his personal qualities but rather for the pattern he

---

versity Press, 1966), annotated; Don Martindale (ed. and trans.),
The Rational and Social Foundations of Music (Carbondale: University of Southern Illinois Press, 1961); *The Theory of Social and
Economic Organization*, trans. A. M. Henderson and Talcott
Parsons (New York: Free Press, 1947); and Gerth and Mills, *op.
cit.*, pp. 196–266. The last reference is the best source of Weber's
personal feelings concerning the threat of rationality.

[17] The most comprehensive treatment of the three types of authority
is in Weber's *The Theory of Social and Economic Organization*,
op. cit., pp. 324–406.

extends. Finally, *rational-legal* authority is based on neither magic nor tradition. It rests on a codified set of rules and procedures that clearly establish what is within the leader's province and what is not. Here the office is crucial and not the man. The office itself is bound not by past customs but by anticipations of future exigencies. Law is fundamental, and as long as the law is respected, the leader will be respected as well.

It is one thing to define ideal types, but quite another to relate them to each other. Weber retained the nineteenth-century German penchant for the particular rather than the general. Although he did define the particular in analytic rather than substantive terms, he was unwilling to take the leap that is involved in constructing more intricate systems of whole societies or even whole organizations.[18] There is a lingering uncertainty in interpreting the man. For example, at some points one infers that the quality of the leadership necessarily infects the operations of the total organization, but, at other points, Weber suggested that even a rigorously bureaucratic organization may have a top-echelon leader who is charismatic, traditional, or rational legal.

And consider the relation of the ideal types to each other. How do they develop into and out of each other over time? Once again Weber was ambiguous. Sometimes he asserted emphatically that he intended no natural development from the charismatic through the traditional to the rational

---

[18] Talcott Parsons has been among Weber's severest critics for this failure of analytic nerve and reluctance to systematize on a large scale, despite the fact that Parsons is among Weber's fondest admirers and perhaps the single most important spark behind Weber's ex post facto surge to prominence in American sociology some fifteen years after his death. See Parsons' introduction to *The Sociology of Religion, op. cit.,* a searching treatment of Weber's virtues and liabilities that is eclipsed only by Parsons' own earlier work, *The Structure of Social Action, op. cit.*

legal.[19] Other times his logic suggested an inexorable progression of just this sort. The case of developing Christianity and Catholicism seems to support the latter, more evolutionary view.

There are, of course, few more shimmering examples of charisma than Jesus. Recently Milton Rokeach recorded the fate of three contemporary figures who claimed to be Christ and who confronted each other in a back ward of a mental hospital.[20] The point is twofold. First, Jesus' own charisma has stood the test of constant emulation. Second, quite apart from what we might do today to a man claiming unique religious gifts, and wholly aside from unceasing debate surrounding Jesus' putative miracles, he was infinitely credible to his followers as one of extraordinary dimensions. Here was a man proclaiming a mission against enormous odds, a mission that sought to impose a new cultural order by altering traditions and structures that gave no signs of yielding easily. The aura of magic and miracles was crucial to both the mission and its wider acceptance. Indeed, in the light of such magic and miracles, the mission became less important than simply following the man.

Yet Weber would be the first to admit that this description oversimplifies the reality. Actually, as much as Jesus conforms to the charismatic image, he also confronts it with two fundamental challenges. First, the above presentation of charismatic, traditional, and rational-legal authority implied that any single leader can invoke one and only one of three legitimations. Jesus suggests the contrary. Although

---

19 One common interpretation of the three types of authority posits traditionalism and rational legality as essentially stable structures, with charisma as a threat to both that may develop at any time.

20 Milton Rokeach, *Three Christs of Ypsilanti* (New York: Knopf, 1964).

he was nothing if not charismatic, he was also legitimated to a lesser extent by both tradition and rationality. Certainly he owed much of his stature to the Judaic prophetic tradition, within which Jesus was neither the first nor the last to vie for divine leadership. Insofar as Jesus alienated the Jews, he did so less because of his personal aberrations and more because of his ideological message. But his leadership also smacked a bit of rationality, again in keeping with Judaism itself. The Talmud was among the first instances of codified religious instruction, and it was within these bounds that Jesus was constrained to operate. His innovations were not so much attacks upon codification itself as efforts to change its ultimate goals and content. The phrase "It is written, but I say unto you . . ." pays respect to a legal order while breaking from it.

In short, it may very well be that the secret of any viable leader is the extent to which he is able to *combine* charismatic, traditional, and rational-legal appeals. Their respective proportions may change as the organization develops and the leadership is challenged by new sorts of emergencies and exigencies. Still, for all the development that we shall describe, it is important to remember that the genius of the Catholic church is precisely its ability to sully and amalgamate the ideal-typical authority patterns. To pursue one pattern to the exclusion of the rest is folly; it may produce sociological elegance, but it is just as likely to produce organizational chaos.

Bearing this in mind, let us return to the concept of charisma and to another issue that Jesus raises. It is possible to read Weber as a leading advocate of the "great-man theory of history," in which exceptional leaders forge new paths for new civilizations on the basis of their personal brilliance and individual magnitude. Certainly the concept of charisma seems to support this view, especially because some regard the concept as the root of Weber's larger theory of social change.[21] But Weber was once again ambiguous, this time to his own advantage. Note that he emphasized not so much what the leader is, but rather the way in which the leader is interpreted by his followers. Charisma itself may be a property less of the man than of the interaction between the man and his adherents; it may even be imputed to the man by adherents who need a leader and are willing to contrive one. The case of Jesus gives surprising substance to this latter possibility. For all his self-conviction, he was a reluctant leader, as indicated in the earlier discussion of his unwillingness to mold a politically aggressive, nationalistic movement in the Judaic pattern. Indeed, Jesus actually seems to have been as humble as the faith he advocated—and humility can be a pronounced liability for the leader of precarious movements. Here was no soapbox spellbinder or swashbuckling religious general. Instead of his claiming all the magical qualities with which he is associated, many were affixed to him by his disciples only after his passing. Thus, much of his charisma was ex post facto and developed to fit the desperate needs of a struggling social movement seeking a symbol around which to galvanize. Biblical scholars have long known that the Gospel accounts grow more spectacular as their date of authorship is further removed from Jesus himself. Mark portrays Jesus as more human and more fallible, attempting to cure all but succeeding for only a few; the

---

[21] Yet Weber also discusses other more gradual sorts of social change that do not depend upon charisma. Certainly he sees rationality itself as a mechanism for producing change as tradition is altered in the sometimes ruthless interests of efficiency. This point is especially clear when he talks about the full-fledged development of capitalism following its own destiny in a near-automated fashion. From Weber's view, this sort of change was pernicious precisely because it left no room for charismatic or cultural appeals.

later accounts of Luke and Matthew are more miraculous as the success rate moves to totality. Jesus was unaware of and unresponsible for such key aspects of Catholic doctrine as the trinity, original sin, and the virgin birth; the crucial notion of a sacerdotal system awaited much later developments in church organization, and the doctrine of the immaculate conception (referring to Mary rather than to Jesus) became official dogma only in 1854 as part of a general surge of Mariolatry. Indeed, a currently prominent interpretation even regards Jesus' denial of status as the "son of God" as more than mere modesty. Apparently, he was sincere in resisting even this most basic of all labels.

This approach suggests, then, that charisma may be imputed as well as claimed and that a single individual may be put to assorted uses by his varied heirs and assigns. Certainly the interpretation given Jesus by his early followers was much different from the aristocratic twists supplied by his medieval flock or even the politicized portrait that emerged out of the Marxist influence on nineteenth-century European Catholicism.

But there is a further implication of the shifting images of Jesus' leadership. A charismatic movement faces a stern crisis when its original leader passes. Weber was especially acute on this point and dealt with it under two rubrics, both of which serve as bridges to traditional authority itself. First, Weber talked of the "routinization of charisma" by which the magical qualities become institutionalized and by which the qualities of the person become generalizable qualities of the movement as a whole. Second, and more specifically, Weber discussed the "charisma of office" as distinct from the "charisma of the individual," suggesting a stage in the routinization at which any occupant of the leadership position is automatically conferred respect because of the qualities ascribed to the position itself. It was not only men like Paul and Augustine who partook of this transference; the contemporary papacy is a clear case in point and was Weber's principal example. Indeed, the doctrine of apostolic succession is a major element in providing charisma for generations of priests and popes alike.

In any event, "charisma of office" suggests a shift away from the magical individual toward traditionalism itself. Here leadership is authenticated and legitimated by past precedent, and again Christianity supplies abundant illustration. Some would argue that Catholicism has been dominated by traditional authority ever since the second century and that its traditionalism is maintained today. To be sure, it has undergone changes in the specific forms of traditionalism. Its initial phase involved a fusion of Christian leadership with the office of the Roman emperor. Later, of course, both the bishopric and the papacy became more autonomous. Concerning this trend, Weber noted the importance of "institutionalizing the dispensation of grace" and building organizational control at the expense of the religious virtuoso. This eclipses charismatic potential within the church but allows the church greater leverage and calculation in herding its flock and tending to its exigencies.

This implication recalls our earlier point that any viable leader is apt to be partly charismatic, partly traditional, and partly rational legal, though the proportions may vary enormously. Although charismatic and traditional features are clearly still present as aspects of Catholic authority, rational-legal authority has also been a party to the leadership proceedings, one whose presence has been increasingly influential since its formal entry with the codification of canon law in the eleventh century. Gradually, the leadership has become highly legalistic and contractual, as has the structure of the Catholic church in general. Much of this rationalization was an unintended response to challenges and opportunities associated with the political and economic affairs of Europe. From this perspective, the church's transition was certainly a success. Catholicism not only gained increasing secular power but was also equipped to weather such later storms as urbanization, nationalism, and the great Western schism of the fourteenth century.[22]

This increasing emphasis on rational authority and bureaucratic structure had its costs as well. It can be argued—as did Weber in other contexts—that even a mild dose of rationality may be fatal to an institution that depends upon an arational mystique for its distinctive identity. Whereas all institutions depend upon arationality (seemingly arbitrary norms and values) to some extent, the church is an extreme case and hence more vulnerable than most to change. As the emphasis shifted from charismatic to traditional and finally to rational-legal organization, Catholicism grew increasingly secular and increasingly expansive in seeking to control formerly nonreligious facets of society. In Durkheim's terms, the sacred invaded the profane, and, as Durkheim might have predicted, the profane retaliated by contaminating the sacred itself. The Dutch historian Johan Huizinga amply documented this trend in his study of Catholicism during "the waning of the Middle Ages." He

---

22 Throughout this chapter, we have put little emphasis on external factors impinging upon the church, factors such as economic change and political machinations. This omission should not suggest that these pressures were absent or that the church was always able to anticipate them instead of becoming unintentionally caught up within them. It is rather that Weber himself spent little time on such variables, partly because of his reaction to Marx, partly because of his reluctance to spin out a theory of society in general, and partly because he made no effort to write a thorough history of Catholicism. The next chapter, however, will raise more of these issues in connection with the rise of Protestantism.

indicated that blasphemy and religious ritual often occupied the same altar; sacred festivals were frequently passed in debauchery, and the church was a common base of solicitation for prostitutes.[23] In one sense, religion and religious dogma were taken for granted. Doctrinal affairs had been eclipsed by the church's political and organizational concerns. Indeed, the doctrine and its miraculous elements had been so codified that faith had been minimized. Jacob Burckhardt noted that the church virtually invited criticism of its dogma so long as these criticisms were not of the church itself.[24] But the line between dogma and church is not easy to draw, and the church was far from immune. In choosing to compete with political and economic institutions on political and economic grounds, the church admitted conditions of battle that were essentially secular. The papacy was under constant siege from its secular opponents, and Catholicism was forced to move in an ever-more-secular direction to meet the demands upon it.

Throughout this movement, we glimpse the operation of a "self-defeating prophecy." That is, as the church defined itself as a rational instrument seeking to control all aspects of society, it lost much of its distinctive mystique and thereby jeopardized not only its potential but even the power it had already attained. The point is not only that the pursuit of "absolute power corrupts absolutely" but also

---

[23] Johan Huizinga, *The Waning of the Middle Ages* (London: St. Martin's Press, 1924), especially pp. 151–224. It should be pointed out that Huizinga himself used a different approach to account for such contaminations—blasphemies that he recoiled from with all the horror of a devoted churchman. Instead of relying upon sociological reasoning, his own explanation is more psychological in arguing that people simply had become religiously satiated so that the mystery of religion had lost its compelling power.

[24] Jacob Burckhardt, *The Civilization of the Renaissance in Italy* (New York: Modern Library, 1954), especially pp. 80–99, 341–381.

that it is dangerous to allow a latent function to become manifest. Catholicism's power play had become all too obvious—and with dire consequences.[25]

The Church-Sect Dynamic and the Rise of Catholicism

There are few formulations in the sociology of religion that have commanded more lip service *and* more serious attention than the distinction between sect and church. Here is an omnibus distinction that covers everything from ministry to membership, from theology to ritual, from social class origins to attitudes toward the surrounding society. On each dimension, the church holds up one end while the sect seesaws on the other. The two organizational models are classic polar types. Later we shall see that the church-sect distinction has been subject to myriad refinements and not a few criticisms. Much of this reassessment is based on the feeling that the dichotomy is too crude in embracing so much and so passionately. True enough, but for this very reason the framework has been provocative, and its expansiveness provides for a convenient summary of the chapter so far.

The distinction between church and sect neither originated with Weber nor received its fullest statement from him.[26] Weber borrowed the usage from a little-known predecessor,

---

25 For elaboration and documentation of this point, see Troeltsch, *op. cit.*; Cohn, *op. cit.*; and J. Milton Yinger, *Religion in the Struggle for Power* (Durham, N.C.: Duke University Press, 1946).

26 Actually Weber rarely elaborates the church-sect distinction at any length. He mentions that the concept was "used at about the same time, and I assume, independently from me, by Kattenbusch . . ." and goes on to give Troeltsch credit for a fuller subsequent discussion. See *The Protestant Ethic and the Spirit of Capitalism, op. cit.*, p. 255.

and certainly men like Ernst Troeltsch,[27] H. Richard Niebuhr,[28] Liston Pope,[29] S. Milton Yinger,[30] and Bryan R.
Wilson[31] have devoted more systematic attention to it.
Nevertheless, Weber put the concept to its most spectacular
deployment in his analysis of the rise of Protestantism, and
the concept is inextricably "his" for the thrust he gave to it.

Without following Weber—or anyone else—too closely in
this matter, we can see the differences between sect and
church from two perspectives, one having to do with the
organizations' internal characteristics and the other involving their external relations with the societal context. *Internally*, the sect features doctrinal purity (though not
necessarily conservatism or fundamentalism), spontaneous
worship with group participation, a lay ministry without
professional pedigree, an explicitly nonbureaucratic organizational structure, and a total ideology of life and ethics
that brooks no compromise and extends its influence into
the members' most mundane activities. By sharp contrast,
the church manifests an evolving doctrine subject to re-

---

[27] Troeltsch, *op. cit.*, especially I, 328–354. But Troeltsch contrasted
both church and sect to still a third type of religious expression:
mysticism. Note, however, that Troeltsch's use of the term departs
from Weber's in a number of respects. Although both saw mysticism as essentially individualistic, Troeltsch pictured it less in
terms of a withdrawn contemplation of the world and more in
terms of active antiassociationalism in which the individual departs
organized religion to go it alone within the world rather than outside it. Thus, Troeltsch predicted that mysticism would become a
dominant form of religion among the well-educated middle classes.
He saw it as a liberalizing spirit within Protestantism that would
eclipse both the church and the sect as religious molds.

[28] H. Richard Niebuhr, *The Social Sources of Denominationalism*
(New York: Holt, Rinehart and Winston, 1929).

[29] Liston Pope, *Millhands and Preachers*, 2nd ed. (New Haven,
Conn.: Yale University Press, 1965), especially pp. 117–140.

[30] Yinger, *op. cit.*

[31] Bryan R. Wilson, "An Analysis of Sect Development," *American
Sociological Review*, 24 (February 1959), 3–15.

interpretation and expected dispute, a highly prescribed and ritualized worship service, a professional priesthood at the top of a hierarchical organizational structure, and a penchant for relative rather than absolute ethics that recognizes possible conflicts and compromises with other ethical demands. *Externally,* the sect is either aloof from or antagonistic toward the prevailing society; it recruits from among the lower classes and disenfranchised elements, but it has exclusive standards of membership that may feature a sharp conversion experience. Again in contrast, the church accommodates the secular society and seeks to work within it. The church practices a universalistic and almost indiscriminate evangelism in that its doors are professedly open to all; but it tends to become the lair of the middle and upper classes, who come to dominate in numbers as well as in influence.

The foregoing merely lists characteristics without forging any causal links between them. This is in the spirit of the Weberian ideal type, but specific causal relationships may be suggested on the basis of some of the more recent research on the distinction cited earlier, that is, Niebuhr, Pope, Yinger, and Wilson, for example. One can argue that the central clue concerns the social class base of the membership. Because the sect is lower class, its appeal rests on providing an exclusive fellowship of the elect for those who are denied access elsewhere and on supplying an ideology of escape and otherworldly salvation for those who find this world oppressive. Much of the sect's emphasis on doctrinal purity and the total ideology is designed to provide a new framework for self-evaluation to those who are evaluated so demeaningly by prevailing standards. Then, too, the explicit disavowal of a professional priesthood and a bureaucratic organization, together with the emphasis on spontaneous individual participation in the worship service, is an alternative to those who find neither niche nor solace in other, more middle-class settings that stress professional competence and administrative skill. A reverse line of reasoning helps to piece together the characteristics of the church. Given its middle-class clientele, the church cannot afford to ask too much of those who are also members of a host of other organizations that exert their own demands and normative requirements. The church must reconcile itself to the secular society, rather than spurn it. It must provide the doctrinal relativity and organizational trappings that have long been associated with middle- and upper-class voluntary associations. A pedigreed priesthood is necessary if there is to be any authority at all. A formal worship service with prescribed rituals delimits the religious experience by putting boundaries around it—and aesthetically appealing boundaries at that.

In any event, the distinction between sect and church has cut a wide swath through the literature on the sociology of religion. As a sensitizing framework, it crops up in study after study of everything from snake-handling cults to Berkeley's Free Speech Movement. Before it is applied to the rise of Christianity and Catholicism, however, one more crucial element must be added: the dynamic interrelatedness between church and sect themselves.[32] Certainly it would be inaccurate to assume that the church and the sect operate entirely independently of one another or that they spring from wholly different wells. In practice, the two are bound together in a kind of cyclical dialectic. Thus, as with Protestantism itself, the typical sect is spawned out of disenchantment with a mother church, and the sect's first-gen-

---

[32] Actually the conception of the "church-sect dynamic" owes more to both Troeltsch and Niebuhr than it does to Weber. Wilson, in *ibid.*, offers a still more probing and more contemporary account that is less a model than a full-scale theory.

eration members are generally the formerly disgruntled members of a church they feel has "sold out" or otherwise betrayed them. The sect galvanizes around a charismatic lay leader and goes its perfervid way until a series of crises begin with the passing of the original leader and the original membership. At this point the sect must ponder its destiny in the face of several stern challenges. Will it replace irreplaceable charisma with a professional priesthood whose credentials at least offer stability? Will it relax its membership criteria so as to ease recruitment among people who never suffered the initial wrongs against which the sect organized in the first place? Will it put a special emphasis on recruiting middle-class types both to confer a stamp of respectability and to attend to the administrative tasks that may have been neglected? Finally, will the sect compromise not only its doctrine but also its ideological aggressiveness in order to decrease society's hostility toward it and increase its recruitment potential?[33] Of course, many sects refuse to take any of these adaptive paths and die out quickly; several take them but disappear nevertheless; some refuse but survive in spite of it; finally, a few adapt and begin the cycle all over again by ultimately spawning their own sects.[34] This last group is classically represented by Catholicism.

---

[33] For a case study of a sect confronting these problems in an intensified context, see Phillip E. Hammond, "The Migrating Sect: An Illustration from Early Norwegian Immigration," *Social Forces*, 41 (March 1963), 275–283.

[34] All this suggests that religious organizations are rational creatures that make purposive decisions in pursuing their individual destinies. Clearly, this is not the case. Such "decisions" to adapt or not are rarely thought out or uttered; most such developments occur unintentionally and after substantial cross-pressuring and trial and error. This is all by way of an apology for the metaphor and an anticipation of charges of "reification"—treating impersonal abstractions as

There is little disagreement that the early Christian movement conformed closely to the sect model, and we have already seen most of the reasons, which range from a radical change in doctrine to a charismatic, nonprofessional leader, from a disenfranchised membership to an emphasis on uncompromising ideology. Christianity also fits the dynamic model of the shift from sect to church. Over time, evangelizing grew more universalistic, and the social class of the membership underwent upward mobility. The movement went to some pains to accommodate the Roman Empire, even to the extent of coopting the emperor himself as a nominal leader. A professional priesthood took little time in appearing, and Catholicism soon flowered as a hierarchical and even authoritarian organizational structure that deemphasized the subjective, individualistic quality of religion and posited instead a highly routinized collective experience. There is no doubt that the changes, however unintended, were in the interests of stability. These changes were precisely the adaptations that were necessary to ensure Catholicism's survival on the slippery social, economic, and political shoals of Europe and the Mediterranean basin.

Note, however, that the move from sect to church had its negative side as well, as we have already glimpsed in the related shifts from charismatic to rational-legal authority and from Christianity as a religion of the dispossessed to elitist Catholicism on the eve of the Reformation. One indication of the difficulties experienced by any church is the number of sect-type splinter movements that are thrown off, and Ernst Troeltsch's tome *The Social Teachings of the Christian Churches* owes much of its length to the job of chronicling the many sects that were involved. These sects

---

if they are actual and intentional "things." As one of our colleagues put it in response to such an allegation: "Only my opponents reify; I simplify."

ranged from the Waldensians to the Franciscans and the Gregorians, not to mention the Protestants, to be discussed in the next chapter.

The more remarkable fact of Catholicism's development is the extent to which it was able to survive these breached and painful births. Indeed, Catholicism was ultimately able to keep most of them in the family. It remains a fair question, however, whether Catholicism survived *in spite of* its abortive insurrections or *because* of them. The latter argument is more plausible than it may seem at first glance. The church was certainly obligated to make small concessions in order to prevent a wholesale splintering. Many of the sects were ultimately incorporated into the church structure as distinctive orders, an ingenious organizational device that kept the central organization intact and on course while making room for the religious mavericks.[35] The Catholic church provides a long series of lessons in the technique of coöptation, that is, the process whereby an existing organization handles its opponents by simply bringing them into the fold. It is sometimes difficult, however, to discern who is coopting whom when the lines of authority become blurred in a merger.

Thus, a fundamental point emerges. Throughout this chapter we have been grappling with the systematic distortions of ideal types, recognizing that no instance of reality is likely to be a perfect reflection of any of the models at issue, certainly not Catholicism, partly because of its penchant for responding to threats by absorbing them. On the one hand, Catholicism is blatantly churchlike in its organizational structure, its rigid ritualism, and its willingness to act

---

[35] A device analyzed in a modern setting by Phillip E. Hammond and Robert E. Mitchell, "Segmentation of Radicalism: The Case of the Protestant Campus Minister," *American Journal of Sociology*, 71 (September 1965), 133–143.

within society in order to change it. On the other hand, one can also argue that Catholicism has retained much of its original sectlike flavor. Its doctrine remains otherworldly as a balm for the dispossessed; it retains a charisma of office that goes far beyond a merely professional priesthood; it continues to advance a total ideology that seeks to penetrate every nook and cranny of the parishioner's life; and, finally, it has retained a substantial lower-class membership despite the periodic waves of anticlericalism that have characterized this group.

This combination of churchlike and sectlike attributes is neither new nor newly noted. Troeltsch argued that much of the dynamics of early Christianity and later Catholicism is due to precisely this mixture and its attendant dialectic. Yinger pointed out that a vascillation between sectlike and churchlike modes is characteristic of any religious movement embarked upon the "struggle for power." Demerath has suggested that the viability of any organization over the long run requires that both churchlike and sectlike needs be met and that a membership drawn from different social classes ensures a division of labor to this end.[36]

Of course this is precisely the kind of thinking that ideal types are supposed to encourage. Weber is clear in his hopes for refinement and even criticism.[37] His hopes have been highly rewarded by the critical efforts of the last two decades. As we shall see in Chapter V, some scholars have argued that the distinction between church and sect should be restricted to the theological differences and should exclude issues concerning the parishioners' social class, church politics, and organizational structure; others have taken the reverse position. Some have expanded the distinction by

---

[36] N. J. Demerath III, *Social Class in American Protestantism* (Chicago: Rand McNally, 1965), pp. 177–204.

[37] Bendix, *op. cit.*, p. 33.

adding new categories, including the cult, the institutionalized sect, the denomination, and the ecclesia. A few have
argued that the cyclical flux from church to sect and back
again is muddied by the ideal types. Several have debated
specific cases, wondering whether such groups as the Methodists, the Presbyterians, and the Baptists are currently
closer to sects or churches. And some have called for the
distinction's demise altogether, pointing not only to its misleading insights on Western religion but also to it irrele-
vance for non-Western, nonorganized religious forms.

Each of these points has merit, but the debate itself has
been a fulcrum for a good deal of the most important
theoretical work in the field. The church-sect distinction has
been an *agent provocateur,* and for some purposes it may be
better to have a false construct that excites reaction than an
irrefutable truth that is ignored.

Two Summaries

In pursuing perspectives on religion in complex
society, we have leaned heavily on one who has been
a crutch for generations of sociologists: Max Weber. Using
early Christianity and the development of Catholicism as a
case in point, we have sought to introduce several Weberian
concepts that have wider applications. Distinctions in theology, prophecy, social class, theodicy, and forms of authority and church versus sect are all central to the Weberian
enterprise, and they are no less important to the sociology
of religion as a whole.

As ideal types, these distinctions offer strategic distortions, designed to sharpen our image of reality precisely by
departing from it. Still, there is a central theme in our own
treatment of these ideal types that is worth final emphasis.
We have suggested at several points that the most stable

organizations are those that straddle Weber's dichotomies and trichotomies, whether combining various social classes in the membership; combining charismatic, traditional, and rational-legal legitimations of authority; or combining churchlike and sectlike attributes. The point can be extended. Successful religious prophets may be either more exemplary or more ethical, but they can ill-afford to be *totally* one or the other. Viable theologies may be either more otherworldly or more this-worldly, either more mystical or more ascetic, but they must have some of all four qualities if their theology is to answer the needs of heterogeneous adherents and cope with various institutional tensions. In short, we must avoid misinterpreting Weber's ideal types as recipes for organizational perfection. Weber performed the task of any successful analyst in pulling reality apart; the task of any successful organization is to put this reality back together again. Early Catholicism offers a model of institutional viability in the face of enormous odds. Its own recipe for stability in the midst of adversity might well be simply to make room for as many seemingly irreconcilable qualities as possible. The Protestant Reformation arose at precisely the point at which Catholicism had moved too far in a number of directions to protect its several exposed flanks.

And yet there is an alternative way of summarizing this chapter by simply listing those whom it is likely to offend. Certainly its religious scholarship will irritate church historians. Its emphasis on theoretical concepts at the cost of theological irreverence may just as certainly alienate those for whom sociology is a threat rather than an independently valid perspective. Finally, sociological theorists may themselves recoil from some of our conceptual liberties, especially those who have their own crystallized interpretation of Weber and may find the present treatment a bowdlerization of a doctrine that enjoys a religious and charismatic status of its own. From one view, such reactions may be unfortunate; from another, they are advantageous. Offensiveness may stir debate, and debate is needed in the sociology of religion as in the sociology of everything else.

But it may be that we are overestimating our impact and resemble the clergyman who was completely dashed when his wife informed him soberly that no, his sermon was *not* guilty of too much levity. To those who are unprovoked and listless, the next section may be more stimulating. Dispute concerning *The Protestant Ethic and the Rise of Capitalism* has been an open wound in the sociological corpus. Its infection has spread throughout the body—and some would argue that it has reached the brain itself. Here is where Weber's assertions concerning the independent influence of ideas in man's affairs are put to their sharpest test. Ironically, many of the assertions continue to ring true though Weber's own supporting evidence has been reduced to rubble.

III

PROTESTANTISM AND CAPITALISM:
Two Developments in Search of a Relationship

 John Maynard Keynes once commented that all of us, in our everyday lives, are the "slaves of some defunct economist," but there is a very real sense in which sociologists have become the slaves of one defunct social theorist. Max Weber offers a personal example of the charisma he wrote about. Although Weber inveighed against cults of personality in the academic community,[1] his own work has rallied followers to an almost mystical extent. This is nowhere more apparent than

---

[1] Max Weber, "Science as a Vocation," in Hans H. Gerth and C. Wright Mills (eds.), *From Max Weber: Essays in Sociology* (New York: Oxford University Press, 1946), pp. 129–156.

in the obeisance sociologists accord to *The Protestant Ethic and the Spirit of Capitalism.*[2] Many sociologists take it as axiomatic that the rise of Protestantism was a "necessary but not sufficient condition" for the rise of capitalism; a few even go further than Weber intended and assert that the Protestant Ethic "caused" the rise of capitalism in the full sense of that epistemologically ambiguous verb.

All this loyalty is cloaked in irony. It is ironic that sociologists should esteem so highly a work that other disciplines criticize so roundly—as we shall see, Weber has both had and been had by his critics among historians, political scientists, economists, and theologians. It is also ironic that Weber's reputation in religion should hang by this early and slender thread largely because his later and more thorough analytic work *The Sociology of Religion*[3] awaited translation until the 1960s. Finally, there is additional irony in that Weber's later work countervened some of his earlier essay. We have already seen that the older Weber placed a great deal of emphasis on theology as a response to the existential needs of different social classes and different life situations; this more Marxian tack seems to oppose Weber's earlier position that theology may goad the emergence of new life situations and new class ideologies. The contradiction is not quite as blatant or as debilitating as this suggests; still, it remains to be confronted, and this is why we have played hob with Weber's own chronology in our treatment of him. Instead of simply tracing his development, we began with his later work to provide both historical and conceptual background for the debate surrounding his earlier thesis.

The present chapter poses five major questions. First,

---

[2] Max Weber, *The Protestant Ethic and the Spirit of Capitalism,* trans. Talcott Parsons (New York: Scribner, 1928).

[3] Max Weber, *The Sociology of Religion,* trans. Ephraim Fischoff (Boston: Beacon Press, 1963).

what is the thesis and, equally important, what isn't it? Second, what have been the criticisms that concern the existence of capitalism prior to the Protestant Reformation and how would Weber reply? Third, what are the attacks concerning the putative effects of Protestantism on capitalism after the Reformation, and, again, what is Weber's rebuttal? Fourth, is there any chance of salvaging Weber's thesis and is there a possibility that Weber's theory may be better than his history? Fifth, what are the links between Weber's early Protestantism and contemporary American religion as these links have been forged by other sociologists and other social historians?

One final word before we enter the controversy. It is no less presumptuous to assay the debate surrounding the rise and consequences of the Protestant Ethic than it was to capsulize the development of early Christianity and the Catholic monolith. What follows is humble history at best, though it may seem overly assertive in the condensation. Here, as before, the important thing is not the history itself, but rather the concepts at play within it. The debate raises issues that go to the heart of the relation between religion and society. Sociology may be best concocted in the crucible of social change, and the Protestant Reformation offers a crucial case study that has received more intensive consideration from wider disciplines than any other we shall confront in this volume.

The Thesis Revisited

Earlier we indicated that Weber's dominant scholarly interest was not religion but the development of rationality in the West—a development he regarded with both horror and fascination. So it is that his essay *The Protestant Ethic and the Spirit of Capitalism* was primarily an attempt to trace the emergence of economic rationality, using religion as a means to that end. The argument in its most concise form is that gradual refinements in Protestant theology from the sixteenth through the eighteenth centuries provided a break with Catholic traditionalism and offered new sanctions and justifications for rational capitalistic enterprise. But let us trace the matter in slightly more detail.

Weber began his analysis on a surprisingly contemporary note. He observed that (as of 1904) Protestants were overrepresented and Catholics underrepresented among "business leaders and owners of capital, as well as the higher grades of skilled labour, and even the higher technically and commercially trained personnel of modern enterprises."[4] The remainder of the book is offered as an explanation, one that begins where our last chapter ended. There we saw that pre-Reformation Catholicism had extended its reach beyond religious affairs into politics and economics, forging alliances with secular elites. Two consequences followed. First, Catholic traditionalism held sway over worldly activities, with its rejection of usury (charging interest on loans) only one example of the fetters Catholicism placed on capitalistic economic ventures. Second, the peasants were not alone in their alienation from the church, because significant portions of the emerging middle classes were also disaffected. It was to the latter that Protestantism catered. By providing theological justification for their mobility strivings and techniques, Protestantism was able to pluck the middle classes out of the jaws of incipient irreli-

---

[4] Weber, *Protestant Ethic, op. cit.,* p. 35. Specific citations will be minimized in the summary to follow. This is not intended as a thorough exegesis, and, after all, Weber's argument is expressed in relatively short compass.

gion and provide them with a motivation that was eminently religious in its own right.

This shift occurred very gradually. Lutheranism was the first tear in the cloak of Catholic dominance, yet the rip was more revealing in its portent than in its accomplishment. It is true that Martin Luther asserted man's independent, unmediated relationship to God. From this view, salvation did not depend upon sacraments or the recommendations of an institutionalized priesthood; its only price was endurance of the work of this world as a devout "calling." Yet this approach was at best an early antecedent of the "spirit of capitalism." Although secular pursuits were no longer base and work was esteemed as a means if not as an end, note that endurance, not success, was the virtue. Luther himself viewed the business world with abhorrence, and Weber suggested that he was more at home with the reactionary Catholics of his day than he would have been with the Protestant capitalists of the eighteenth century.

Moreover, Lutheranism soon lost its flavor as a rebellious movement. It won an early victory over Catholicism in northern Europe but then began to ape its predecessor, following the classic model of the sect-church dynamic. Sacraments, priestly hierarchies, and institutionalized ritual all arose at the expense of religious individualism, and John Calvin emerged to stem the Protestant reversion. As if to complete what Luther had started, Calvin sought to renew the attack on churchly appurtenances and to remedy the logical inconsistencies in the budding Protestant theology.

One of the fundamentals of this theology was its premise that God was wholly transcendent and wholly unknowable. It was precisely this premise that undercut the role of the church as intermediary. But, Calvin argued, if the church is unable to fathom or manipulate the ways of God, why is the individual apt to be more successful? How could one be sure of salvation if God was indeed unknowable and un-predictable? How could one rest assured that endurance of one's calling was sufficient? This questioning led Calvin to a theodicy that was as logically elegant as it was ethically unsatisfactory: Salvation was wholly predestined, and the individual had neither a choice nor a clue.

Weber was clear in indicating that just as Luther was more at home with the Catholic economic conservatives, Calvin was also far from the full-blown Protestant Ethic. Yet the doctrine of predestination put an even greater premium on ethical individualism because the individual was completely adrift with no assurances and no real insti-tutional support. Moreover, Calvin's view of predestination made the whole issue of salvation much more problematic. Both Catholicism and Lutheranism had virtually guaran-teed salvation to those who mind their religious manners. Calvin argued that even the most devout and circumspect adherent could never be sure. Two further refinements were to follow that would violate Calvin's own logic in the interest of a more workable ethic, one that changed the theological conception of work itself.

The first of these innovations arose through the writings of such theologians as Beza and Zinzendorf. Briefly, this developing argument was that although predestination is indeed immutable, clues are available. One need not abide with only a hope and a prayer, because it is possible to discern the possibilities of salvation in the life to come by observing one's success in this life. The definition of "suc-cess" here was obviously crucial, and it turned on a new formulation. No longer was work merely a calling to be endured; now it was seen as a glorification of God and more of an end in itself. The successful worker was the successful servant, and money became a metric for the measurement of grace.

From here it was only a skip of the pen and a loose hermeneutic metaphor to the final theological development —one that capped the Protestant Ethic by under-cutting predestination itself. With men like England's Richard Baxter, the doctrine evolved to the point that worldly success was not merely a sign of salvation but actually a way of *earning* it. Thus, work became still more important, and economic success became a ticket into the parlor of the elect. Here is the spirit of capitalism in its full flower, with religious motivation as a crucial bulwark for economic zeal. Not only was the individual encouraged to pursue his fortune, but fortune seeking became a nobly legitimate undertaking. This is not to say that the new ethic put a premium on wealth for wealth's sake or on self-indulgent acquisitiveness. Weber cited Benjamin Franklin as well as John Wesley on the virtues of penny pinching and, in effect, the desirability of plowing the profits back into the firm. Indeed, it was precisely the combined admonitions to make profits and then to plow them back that was basic to the rise of capitalistic enterprise. Here lay the spur to economic growth and planning that was crucial to rational capitalism as a whole.

By this time, then, the hegemony of Catholic traditionalism had given way to a new set of values and, in turn, to a new economic system. In theological terms, otherworldly asceticism had been eclipsed by an active, this-worldly asceticism in the interest of controlling the world and manipulating one's own destiny. The thesis puts the lie to a Marxian materialistic conception of history and shows the importance of ideas and values as independent forces rather than mere historical epiphenomena.

But this last point requires qualification in Weber's own terms. Unhappily, his essay is often misunderstood as asserting the unilinear and exclusive influence of Protestantism in the rise of capitalism. It is true, of course, that the essay was partly designed as a rebuttal to Marx. At the same time, Protestantism was only one among many factors involved—it was "necessary but not sufficient"— and Weber's last words are the following:

> . . . *it is, of course, not my aim to substitute for a one-sided materialistic an equally one-sided spiritualistic causal interpretation of culture and of history. Each is equally possible, but each, if it does not serve as the preparation, but as the conclusion of an investigation, accomplishes equally little in the interest of historical truth.*[5]

This tack was clearly meant to allay those waiting to chide Weber for a naïve idealism, and, as we saw earlier, he moved even further toward a Marxian rapprochement in his later work. Still, criticisms abound and many are especially devastating for debating not what the facts should be but what they actually are.

The Case for Pre-Reformation Capitalism

Criticisms of the Weber thesis can be divided into two groups, one concerning the existence of both capitalism and religious incentives for it prior to Protestantism and the other challenging the post-Reformation effects of Protestantism itself. The second will be discussed in the

---

[5] *Ibid.*, p. 183. At this point it should be noted that we are committing a major, though calculated, offense in assessing Weber's argument for western Europe without reference to his efforts to extend the case comparatively in his analyses of *Ancient Judaism, The Religion of India,* and *The Religion of China.* These works (cited in the previous chapter) are, if anything, more impressive than the analysis of the Protestant case. They should certainly be considered in any thorough assessment of Weber, and we have omitted them only because we have no illusions of thoroughness and have sought to focus on historical developments in the West alone.

next section. Meanwhile, the first is given theme and coun-
terpoint by a host of scholars, most of whom have their own
favorite examples of early capitalists and early Catholic
theologians who were sympathetic.

Let us consider a few of these and try to imagine what
Weber's rebuttal might have been. For instance, the distinguished economic historian Henri Pirenne tells us of one
Saint Godric of Finchale as a case in point. Godric was an
eleventh-century peasant who took to beachcombing and
peddling the remains of ships wrecked off the coast of
England. A clever fellow, he pyramided his capital and
gradually worked his way upward within ever-larger organizations of merchants until finally he was a major figure in
the trade between England, Flanders, and Denmark. In
Pirenne's own words, "At the end of several years this
prudent custom of buying cheap and selling dear made of
Godric a very rich man. It was then that, moved by grace,
he suddenly renounced the life he had led until then,
turned over his possessions to the poor, and became a
hermit."[6]

Weber's reply might be surmised from his rebuttals to
similar cases offered by his contemporaries. First, note that
Godric was consumed with contrition for his enterprise,
that he felt compelled to renounce his life and possessions,
and that, "moved by grace," he later became a hermit (and
then a monk). It is clear that his capitalism was religiously
illegitimate and a breach of traditional economic values.
Weber did not deny that such ventures occurred but asserted only that they were illicit until actually championed
by the theological developments of Protestantism. Second,
however, Weber would argue that this is not the sort of

---

[6] Henri Pirenne, *Medieval Cities* (Princeton, N.J.: Princeton University Press, 1925), p. 82.

capitalism at issue in his essay. He distinguished between capitalism as a generic form and the "rational capitalism" that was peculiar to Western Europe after the Reformation. The distinction is crucial, and it is worth recalling Weber's own words:

> *The impulse to acquisition, pursuit of gain, of money, of the greatest possible amount of money, has in itself nothing to do with capitalism. This impulse exists and has existed among waiters, physicians, coachmen, artists, prostitutes, dishonest officials, soldiers, nobles, crusaders, gamblers, and beggars. . . . [Even in the sense of rationally calculated money transactions] capitalism and capitalistic enterprises . . . have existed in all civilized countries of the earth. . . . However, trade especially was for a long time not continuous like our own, but consisted essentially in a series of individual undertakings. Only gradually did the activities of even the large merchants acquire an inner cohesion (with branch organizations, etc.). In any case, the capitalistic enterprise and the capitalistic entrepreneur, not only as occasional but as regular entrepreneurs, are very old and very widespread. . . . But in modern times the Occident has developed, in addition to this, a very different form of capitalism which has appeared nowhere else: the rational capitalistic organization of (formally) free labour.*[7]

Note then that Weber's distinctive conception of "rational capitalism" depends upon the existence of rational *organization*, which can in turn be seen in terms of the characteristics of Weberian "bureaucracy"—specialized, impersonal, calculating, hierarchical, and based on universalistic rather than particularistic judgments of policies and manpower.[8]

---

[7] Weber, *Protestant Ethic, op. cit.,* pp. 17–21.
[8] See Gerth and Mills, *op. cit.,* pp. 196–244 and Max Weber, *The Theory of Social and Economic Organization* (New York: Oxford University Press, 1947), pp. 324–341.

Time and again, Weber repaired to the distinction between types of capitalism. For example, the distinction was also a key factor in Weber's defense against the thesis of a colleague, Werner Sombart, that the Jews were most instrumental in promoting Western capitalism.[9] Weber argued that the Jews were primarily involved in "speculative pariah-capitalism" involving "war, Government contracts, State monopolies, speculative promotions, and the construction and financial projects of princes, which they themselves condemned."[10] This was not the "bourgeois organization of labor" that was at the heart of Puritan or rational capitalism.

Weber used similar reasoning in replying to those who argued that there was Catholic religious support for economic innovation prior to the Reformation. Sombart told of one Leon Batiste Alberti, who in 1450 wrote a document on "holy housekeeping" that might have been modeled after the later Ben Franklin's strictures.[11] Felix Rachfahl pointed out that the Benedictines, the Franciscans, and the Jesuits all rivaled the Puritans in their hospitality toward capitalism in general and even usury in particular.[12] And a contemporary Swedish historian, Kurt Samuelsson, seems to apply the clinchers. He indicates that capitalistic goadings are blatant in the Aristotelian wing of the scholastics and argues that men like Anselm, Abelard, Benard, Lombard, and Bonaventura all expressed sympathy with capitalism

[9] Werner Sombart, *The Jews and Modern Capitalism* (New York: Free Press, 1951).

[10] Weber, *Protestant Ethic, op. cit.*, p. 271.

[11] Werner Sombart, *Der Bourgeois* (Munich, 1913), pp. 136 ff. Cited in Kurt Samuelsson, *Religion and Economic Action: A Critique of Max Weber* (New York: Harper Torchbooks, 1964), p. 63.

[12] Felix Rachfahl, in *Internationale Wochenschrift für Wissenschaft, Kunst und Technik*, Nos. 39–43 (1909); cited by Samuelsson, *op. cit.*, p. 11. According to Samuelsson, Rachfahl was "the first to bring Weber's theories into serious discussion . . ."

prior to the end of the thirteenth century.[13] Moreover, Samuelsson points to the exhortations of a French Catholic, Jacques Savary, published in 1675; here was no isolated crank but a man whose publications rivaled our own Norman Vincent Peale's in number and circulation. Finally, Samuelsson throws salt in the wound by citing seemingly Puritan urgings that date not only from 1610 but from Japan.

Weber would reply again that these were exhortations to capitalism but not to rational capitalism. However, Samuelsson's counterreply as a historian exemplifies a contempt that few sociologists would direct at Weber. In responding to a three-page footnote that Weber wrote for a later edition of his essay—a footnote concerning Alberti and Sombart's original challenge[14]—Samuelsson states:

> *Weber's retaliatory note abounds with sophistries, distortions and circular arguments. It may suffice, by way of a summary of the foregoing, to bring out the following points: (1) that Alberti's rationalism is challenged, only to be declared unchallengeable shortly thereafter—though, by contrast with Franklin's, of no account in the affairs of men; (2) that crucial importance is attached to insignificant divergencies of phraseology between Alberti and Franklin, while little weight is attributed to the similarities in the central theme which, considering the gap in time and environment, are very great; (3) that these divergencies—which may be rightly or wrongly conceived by Weber—are freely interpreted "capitalistically" for Franklin but "non-capitalistically" for Alberti; (4) that the rational, capitalistic temper (which in one place is stated to*

---

13 Samuelsson, *op. cit.* This is, by all odds, the most thorough and devastating critique of Weber the historian, though Samuelsson might be accused of innocently overlooking Weber's theoretical concerns and throwing out the sociological baby with the historical bathwater.

14 Weber, *Protestant Ethic, op. cit.*, pp. 194–198.

> *occur only among the Puritans and in Franklin, while in*
> *another it is declared to occur in Alberti as well but to*
> *affect human conduct only with Puritanism and Franklin)*
> *is presumed to derive only from the unique religious*
> *factor. A period of over 300 years, and wholly different*
> *environments and climates of social opinion: these appar-*
> *ently play no role in the discrepancies alleged by Weber.*
> *Only Franklin's heritage of Puritanism is admitted in ex-*
> *planation of the fact that he expresses himself differently*
> *on a number of points from Alberti writing more than 300*
> *years earlier.*[15]

Thus, in Samuelsson's view, Weber splits hairs to avoid contact with the scalp itself. Other aspects of Samuelsson's thorough critique will occupy us later. Meanwhile, how is the present dispute to be evaluated? Was there a suitably rational capitalism prior to the Reformation and were the Catholics sufficiently prodding to belie the traditionalism with which Weber saddles them?

There is no doubt that Weber overstated the case; it is clear too that his conceptual distinctions were often convenient in their obfuscations just as his historical scholarship was frequently facile in its oversimplification. At the same time, it seems indisputable that rational capitalism underwent a pronounced surge in the three centuries following the Reformation and that prior Catholic sympathies were "represented in but not representative of" the pre-Protestant European scene. If even this much may be granted, the crucial issue becomes one long familiar to even introductory students of statistics: what is the relation between correlation and causation? To say that the rise of Protestantism coincided with a spurt in capitalism is not to say that the two are causally linked either in the direction of Weber's thesis or in line with a more Marxian interpretation

---

[15] Samuelsson, *op. cit.*, p. 64.

that capitalism produced Protestantism itself. Let us examine the issue in more detail by inspecting the debate surrounding post-Reformation developments. Weber's head remains high, if not lofty, but some of the sharpest blows have yet to be struck.

The Post-Reformation Scene: Whither Causality?

〽 One of the most persistent themes among Weber's critics has been that Protestantism was not as sympathetic to capitalism as Weber supposed. Of course, Weber covered himself to some extent in acknowledging the economic conservatism of Luther and Calvin; he even argued that the crucial later developments occurred, for the most part, with no specific economic intent, since men like Beza, Baxter, and John Wesley were responding to theological rather than economic imperatives. Still, Beza, Baxter, and Wesley are part of only a handful of later Protestant thinkers who are basic to Weber's case. Criticism trumps these names with countless others who are alleged to be more representative in their conservatism; many critics even dispute the capitalistic implications of Weber's own star witnesses. Scholars like Winthrop S. Hudson,[16] Henri See,[17] R. H. Tawney,[18] and Richard L. Means[19] are

---

[16] Winthrop S. Hudson, "Puritanism and the Spirit of Capitalism," *Church History*, 18, (March 1949), 3–16; included in Robert W. Green (ed.), *Protestantism and Capitalism: The Weber Thesis and Its Critics* (Boston: Heath, 1959), pp. 46–62. Green's collection serves an important purpose admirably in bringing together a host of divergent views for the reader's inspection.

[17] Henri See, "The Contribution of the Puritans to the Evolution of Modern Capitalism," in Green, *op. cit.*, pp. 62–64.

[18] R. H. Tawney, *Religion and the Rise of Capitalism* (Baltimore: Penguin Books, 1937).

[19] Richard L. Means, "Protestantism and Economic Institutions: Auxiliary Theories to Weber's Protestant Ethic," *Social Forces*, 44 (March 1966), 372–381. Means points out that many of the early

but a few who have attacked from this position. The attack has been sufficiently successful to provoke a search for alternative explanations by those feeling that there was actually something to explain—that is, by those agreeing that capitalism had indeed undergone a surge that began roughly with the Reformation.

Some of these alternatives are true to the Weberian spirit if not to the Weberian letter. Several argue that Protestantism had an impact, but one that was much less direct than in Weber's version. For example, quite apart from any inherently pro- or anti-capitalistic theology, the developments of Protestantism did lead to a new emphasis on rational calculability in general and education in particular. Education was undeniably important to the capitalistic enterprise, especially as Weber defined it. But such a chain of influence does not depend on any natural affinity between Protestantism and capitalism per se. Similar arguments have been advanced for the relationship between Protestantism and the rise of science, with its contribution to capitalism.[20] At this point, however, a new twist is added. Protestants were in many circumstances a put-upon minority in desperate need of legitimation and mobility. Science helped to satisfy both needs and thus may be accountable through the social and not the theological aspects of Protestantism.

This emphasis on the minority status of the early Protestants occurs in still another alternative, one that is not necessarily incompatible with the foregoing. Because the Protestants were a middle-class minority in many European

---

Protestant clergymen were more interested in restraining and reforming capitalism than in goading it on to greater and more oppressive heights.

20 For a classic statement here, see Robert K. Merton, "Puritanism, Pietism, and Science," in his *Social Theory and Social Structure*, rev. ed. (New York: Free Press, 1957), pp. 574–606.

countries, there was a tendency for them to migrate to more hospitable climes. Because the minority was biggest and politically most successful in England, the migration was largely in this direction. It is no accident that capitalism burgeoned first in England, because that country had the advantage of a steady influx of trained middle-class personnel from areas such as France, Italy, Germany, the Netherlands, and Scandinavia. This account is another that carries no necessary assumption that Protestantism was itself conducive or receptive to capitalism. Protestantism's economic ethic may have played at most a minimal role in attracting middle-class members already alienated from Catholicism. Once attracted to the fold, the middle class's natural capitalistic proclivities may have done the rest regardless of theology.

Two other alternatives also make strategic use of Protestantism in a non-Weberian fashion. One of these is a political explanation that is touched upon by the earlier suggestion that the English Puritans won rather quick political success so as to secure the country as a Protestant haven of sorts. Because the Puritan conception of God was so transcendent and so all-powerful, it was difficult for the Puritans to countenance any rival earthly authority. There was, therefore, a premium placed on liberty that involved loosening the bonds of the state on individual behavior in all areas. This attitude was certainly a crucial element in Cromwell's revolt and in the ultimate demise of the English Catholic state, but it had ramifications elsewhere as well. Germany, Scandinavia, and even the countries in central and southern Europe also experienced a gradual relaxation in the power of the state as a conservative agency. In the process, economic control was generally reduced so that capitalism was allowed to gain momentum with minimal interference. According to this formulation, Protestantism could have had an important indirect effect on capitalism even though the capitalists themselves were non-Protestant. That is, the Reformation's primary impact may have been on the broader social and political structure rather than directly on the individual.

Regarding individuals, still another alternative stresses Protestantism's impact on the lower classes rather than the middle classes. Weber's argument, of course, was that Puritanism offered motivation and legitimation to the capitalists themselves, but others indicate that it made at least an equal impact on their employees.[21] The point is well made by two recent sociological accounts of eighteenth- and nineteenth-century industrial development in England. Both Reinhard Bendix[22] and Neil J. Smelser[23] show that whether or not Methodism provided a goad to the bourgeoisie, it was certainly effective in providing a sop for the proletariat. Thus, Bendix described the Society for Promoting Christian Knowledge as a churchly trade school with the purpose of producing obedient workers and servants to fulfill their duties in the "Christian fashion"—a fashion that was tied to a status quo dictated by "divine providence." Precisely because of the Protestant work ethic, it was important as a controlling mechanism among the "free laborers" so vital to Weber's own conception of the rational capitalistic enterprise.

---

[21] Note that this argument seems to imply that the social class composition of the early Protestant groups was heterogeneous. In part, this was the case, and certainly more the case than Weber's treatment would indicate. At the same time, much of Protestantism's influence among the lower classes was communicated through separate mission activities that had minimal contact with a given church's own parish and parishioners.

[22] Reinhard Bendix, *Work and Authority in Industry* (New York: Harper Torchbooks, 1963), especially Chapter 2.

[23] Neil J. Smelser, *Social Change in the Industrial Revolution* (Chicago: University of Chicago Press, 1959).

Each of the preceding alternatives to the Weber thesis has remained true to Protestantism itself as a causal factor in the rise of capitalism. But two final alternatives go further in departing from Weber even in this respect. One holds that Protestantism was at best an ambiguous subcurrent in the real tide of change, the Enlightenment. Gladys Bryson argues that it was this new form of secular liberalism that emancipated and transformed capitalism, not only in Britain but in northern Europe and the United States as well.[24] Indeed, Weber's dependence on Benjamin Franklin is highly misleading, because Franklin was much more representative of the areligious spirit of the Enlightenment than of the intensely religious fervor of the Puritans. Franklin was one of the first American infidels, one who retained a steadfast belief in God but who preferred to interpret ethical mandates in his own fashion while avoiding entanglement with the churches themselves. Nor was Franklin uncharacteristic in this respect. Andrew Carnegie, perhaps the most celebrated folk hero of nineteenth-century American capitalism, had little but contempt for religious creeds of all sorts.[25]

This interpretation may seem a severe rebuttal to Weber the historian, but it is not necessarily an upbraiding for Weber the theorist. To say that the Enlightenment rather than Protestantism paved the way for the rise of capitalism leaves Weber's larger theoretical position intact. Changes in ideas and values *do* make an independent difference and may often be causal agents for changes in material condi-

---

24 See the discussion of Bryson's work and its implications in Samuelsson, *op. cit.*, especially p. 51.

25 See *ibid.*, pp. 67–79, for a general debunking of the notion that the leaders of early American capitalism subscribed to any version of the Protestant Ethic. Samuelsson exposes the areligion in William Graham Sumner, Henry Ford, and others, as well as in Carnegie.

tions and the social structure. This, of course, was the major element in Weber's self-conscious departure from Marxian theory. If even this much can be salvaged, Weber might have been happy, for his allegiances to Protestantism were purely analytic and his historical research was simply a means to a theoretical end.

Yet there is a final alternative account of the age that attacks Weber on theoretical as well as historical grounds. This is perhaps the most obvious alternative of all, one that has been a constant feature of the debate since its inception. Thus, instead of the Protestant Ethic serving as a causal factor in the rise of capitalism, it may have been the reverse: the rise of capitalism caused the emergence of the Protestant Ethic. This, of course, is the Marxian interpretation, championing the causal salience of economic conditions and regarding ideas and values as mere reflections of these conditions. Although the position has always had the support of Marxists, it has had others in its corner as well, and it would be foolish to dismiss this position as mere ideology advanced by mere ideologists. For example, its most recent and perhaps most reasonable statement comes from Kurt Samuelsson,[26] a historian who also subscribes to the Bryson thesis concerning the secularizing impact of the Enlightenment and who is, therefore, willing to see that *some* ideas and *some* values may also be influential.

If, however, developments in Protestant theology were more the results than the cause of capitalism, how might this situation have come about? A large part of the case turns on the relation between the theologian and his audience, between the clergyman and his parishioners. Weber's original essay tended to treat theological developments as

---

[26] This is especially clear in Samuelsson's remarks concerning H. M. Robertson, the leading scholarly exponent of the Marxist position in the debate over Protestantism and capitalism.

part of an internal dialectic of ideas in which logical inconsistencies were corrected for their own sake. He devoted a
great deal of time to theology but relatively little to the
forces at work either on the theologians or on the lesser
clergy who translated the message into pulpit pronouncements intended for the laity.[27] It is apparent, however, that
the laity was more than a captive and passive audience.
One of the consequences of Protestantism itself was to
make the clergy more vulnerable to parishioner demands
both through the deemphasis of the clergy's sacramental
trappings and because of the emphasis on religious individualism with "every man his own priest." Thus, many of
the theological developments were traceable to the demands of the adherents; the doctrine of Protestantism
evolved to satisfy, justify, and rationalize many economic
activities already underway. Samuelsson put the matter this
way in commenting on Baxter, one of Weber's prime witnesses in behalf of the final full flowering of Puritanism's
capitalistic ethic:

> *More interesting than the passages in which Baxter can
> best be described as purely anti-capitalistic are those
> where he takes a more benevolent view of the operations
> of businessmen and entrepreneurs. For it is here that there
> emerges most clearly the dilemma between religion and
> economic activity, in which Baxter and the other Puritan
> fathers found themselves. What we find is not a religious
> teaching urging disciples to address themselves to trade
> and other forms of enterprise and to win God's favour by
> success in such activities; on the contrary, it is a leader of
> the congregation finding that the disciples already con-*

---

27 Indeed, Reinhard Bendix has commented that Weber's work generally suffered from neglect of the issue of individual involvement.
It is ironic that Weber should be remembered for stressing the
importance of "meaning" at the individual level, but his lack of
attentiveness to this level is a sore spot in his analyses. See Bendix, *Max Weber: An Intellectual Portrait* (Garden City, N.Y.:
Doubleday, 1960), especially Chapter VIII.

verted or receptive to his evangelical message consist very largely of businessmen and industrialists. Sensing the claims of practical life, he seeks to resolve the predicament by clarifying the moral conditions under which a prosperous, even wealthy, businessman may, despite success and wealth, become a good Christian.[28]

Weber is not totally without reply. He was cautious to avoid an argument of single causes and more than willing to admit that there was an interaction between economic and noneconomic factors contributing to both the Protestant Ethic and the spirit of capitalism. For example, one plausible defense of Weber in the midst of this salvo is to argue that Protestantism did indeed emerge partially as a response to capitalists' demands, but, once developed, Protestant theology gave these demands further motivation and legitimation on a wider scale. It may very well be that clergymen such as Baxter evolved their theology to please a few prominent parishioners. The crucial point is that the theology itself then took on an independent force of its own.

Even this defense has its detractors. It assumes again that Protestant parishioners were generally pliant and attentive and that Protestant theology was taken seriously enough to affect a change in their view of the world and their approach to success within it. There is evidence that this was rarely the case and that churchgoers more often found the theology insignificant or actually offensive. The distinguished British historian R. H. Tawney commented as follows on the sometimes diffident and sometimes stubborn manner of the Geneva business leaders:

The prosperous bourgeoisie who governed Geneva had no objection to discouraging extravagance in dress, or to

---

[28] Samuelsson, *op. cit.*, p. 28.

exhorting the public to attend sermons and to send their children to catechism. But they heard denunciations of covetousness without enthusiasm, and on two matters they were obdurate. They refused to check, as the ministers concerned to lower prices had demanded, the export of wine, on the ground that it was needed in order to purchase imports of wheat; and, as was natural in a body of well-to-do creditors, they would make no concession to the complaint that debtors were subjected to a "double usury," since they were compelled to repay loans in an appreciating currency.[29]

This statement, to be sure, concerns only the "prosperous bourgeoisie" and only at one time and place. Still, Tawney was confident in generalizing the point, and not without reason. We shall see later that there are significant slips between the theological cup and the laity's lips in the present day. One suspects that this was also true in the sixteenth, seventeenth, and eighteenth centuries, even if to a slightly lesser extent.

Certainly there is evidence that Protestantism's theological distinctiveness was of little significance in the nineteenth century, despite Weber's beginning point that Protestants were overrepresented and Catholics underrepresented in circles of capitalistic prominence by the end of the nineteenth century. Samuelsson reserved some of his most devastating and ingenious criticism for precisely this claim.[30] He argues that, although it is true that northern European countries were generally both more heavily Protestant and more successfully capitalistic than southern European nations, this situation is best explained in terms of natural trade routes and an economic thrust that can be traced back to before the Reformation. Moreover, there are exceptions

---

[29] Tawney, *op. cit.,* p. 107.
[30] Samuelsson, *op. cit.,* pp. 137–150.

to the general premise, for Catholic Belgium developed rational capitalism even before Protestant England, and, within each country, it can be shown that it is frequently the Jews and the Catholics who fare better than the Protestants themselves. This last point takes us to a more specific issue that is especially revealing. Weber relied heavily on statistics for Baden between 1892 and 1898 to show that Protestants had higher income, higher occupational status, and higher education than Catholics. Samuelsson returned to the sources to impugn them thoroughly. Although it is true that Protestants were more often artisans and skilled workers and Catholics were more typically master trades-men in handicraft work, the assumption does not follow that the Catholics were any less inclined to capitalism, for the trades were actually more conducive to capitalistic development. In comparisons of wealth and education, the differences are misleading because they are largely artifacts of the Protestants' greater concentration in urban areas. If one looks at urban residents alone, the differences vanish, because Protestants do not take any greater advantage of educational or economic opportunities when they are available. Samuelsson concludes pointedly by noting that statistics like these could also be used to demonstrate the effects of race and climate on capitalism.

The impact of this critique is lessened only by some of Weber's own words that reduce the importance of the nine-teenth-century data altogether. One sign that the original essay was written quickly is that Weber began by leaning heavily on contemporary evidence but concluded by indicating that the impact of Protestantism had passed and that capitalism had evolved its own autonomous value system, one that no longer required religious reinforcements:

> *In Baxter's view the care for external goods should only lie on the shoulders of the saint like a light cloak, which can*

> *be thrown aside at any moment. But fate decreed that the*
> *cloak should become an iron cage. . . . To-day the spirit*
> *of religious asceticism . . . has escaped from the cage. But*
> *victorious capitalism, since it rests on mechanical founda-*
> *tions, needs its support no longer . . . and the idea of*
> *duty on one's calling prowls about in our lives like the*
> *ghost of dead religious beliefs.*[31]

Weber did not date the end of Protestantism's influence, so
one does not know at what point the absence of Protestant-
Catholic differences becomes a valid criticism. It should be
clear enough that he envisaged few differences for our own
day, and yet, as we shall see later, scholars continue to
"test" his hypothesis by looking for current gaps between
Protestants and Catholics with respect to many and diverse
phenomena, ranging from economic behavior to fertility.[32]
Surely Weber should be spared this much. His thesis was
restricted to a vague but nonetheless limited period. It has
been amply attacked within those confines and to heap
illegitimate on legitimate abuse is unnecessary.

Sectarianism, Secularization, and Differentiation: Weber Reconstructed

Once asked the purpose of his scholarship, Weber
responded, "I want to see how much I can stand."
Certainly sociology has more to recommend it than a test of

---

31 Weber, *Protestant Ethic, op. cit.,* pp. 181–182.

32 For a good summary of this literature, see Andrew M. Greeley,
"The Protestant Ethic: Time for a Moratorium," *Sociological
Analysis,* 25 (Spring 1964), 20–33. There is an old cartoon concerning the fellow who lost a half-dollar in the middle of the
block but searched for it under the corner lightpost because he
could see better there. Alas, there is a sense in which this approach
applies to the sociologists' search for the truth in Weber's argument. Not being historians, we have sought to check the argument
for the twentieth century instead of the sixteenth. The light
may be better for the twentieth, but the argument applies here
neither in its original theory nor in any current fact.

character and endurance, but the question now is how much criticism Weber's *thesis* can stand and still be salvageable. Clearly, it has been attacked from all angles: by those who argue that there was nothing to explain and by those who explain it in different terms, by those who assert that Protestantism made its impact in a wholly different fashion and by those who argue that it had no impact at all and was a symptom rather than a cause. But if Weber's critics agree that he was wrong, they do not agree on what is right. The issue remains moot, and what follows is yet another effort, but with no illusions of definitiveness. It is our conviction that Weber's historical interpretation has obfuscated his theoretical insights and that there is indeed something worth saving in the formulation if not in the facts.

Let us begin then with two concepts that seem to be antithetical. First, "sectarianism" connotes an intensification of religion as new sects proliferate and promote their own distinctive doctrines feverishly. Second, "secularization" implies a watering-down of religion, a contamination of the sacred by the ordinary. It is true that the two concepts stand at opposite poles from the standpoint of the sect members themselves. On the other hand, the two may be complimentary and even causally related from the standpoint of the wider society, particularly when the sects arise to question the validity of a mother church whose ideology has heretofore dominated society in all its facets. Thus, instead of arguing that Protestantism helped pave the way for capitalism by spinning out a legitimating ethic of its own, it may be more accurate to indicate that Protestantism was crucial in simply breaking the yoke of traditional Catholic dominance.

Surely Weber and most of his critics would agree that pre-Reformation Catholicism was inhospitable to any rapid

surge of rational capitalism. It is true enough that the
Benedictines, the Franciscans, and the Jesuits had made
concessions, but these were minority orders within the
church, and we saw earlier that part of the genius of Catholicism has been its ability to make room for its dissidents
by turning them into orders and restricting them to the
sidelines. In any event, if Catholicism in the main posed an
obstacle to the innovations of capitalism, how was the
obstacle to be overcome? Weber's account simply substitutes a new religious ethic for an old one, but our argument
assumes less and may explain more. Instead of emphasizing
the emergence of a religious asceticism as a goad to capitalism, it posits a retrenching of religious control generally so
that capitalism was able to follow its own lead without
constraint. This does not deny that Protestantism had an
impact; rather, it locates this impact in a different place.
Protestantism may have paved the way for capitalism not
because of its theology but *regardless* of its theology. The
important thing was not a change in religion itself but
rather an eclipse of religious influence altogether.

It is in this sense that sectarianism may lead to secularization, and the crucial intervening variable is one of *differentiation.* Thus, the emergence of Protestantism led to a
differentiation in the religious sphere; the ensuing competition fostered a sense of religious relativism by which all
religion lost the sense of compelling immediacy and credibility that Catholicism had enjoyed previously. And as
particular religions were differentiated from each other,
religion in general was differentiated from other realms of
society. Political, educational, and economic activities all
took on new autonomy in the bargain. It was precisely this
autonomy that paved the way for new political freedom (as
witnessed especially in England after Cromwell), new intellectual freedom (as seen in the secularism of the Enlighten-

ment), and, of course, new economic freedom. Yet the term "freedom" is misleading. More accurately, each of these realms, once released from religious restraint, was able to respond more directly to other changes under way—changes such as urbanization, democratization, and increased literacy.

This explanation should not be construed as a complete break with all previous interpretations of the Reformation. We saw earlier that Weber's protégé Troeltsch viewed original Protestantism as neither a sect nor a church. Instead, he saw it as an example of still a third form of religion, one that he termed "mysticism," using the word in quite a different fashion from Weber:

> *Finally, we must not forget that . . . the growth of an independent lay civilization in the cities, itself created a powerful competition with the previous world of thought, which had been controlled by the Church and particularly by the priests. Its first effect was naturally to limit the power of the ecclesiastical civilization. . . . Through all of these movements, however, a sociological type of Christian thought was being developed, which was not the same as that of the sect-type; it was, in fact, a new type—the radical religious individualism of mysticism. This type had no desire for an organized fellowship. . . . The isolated individual, and psychological abstraction and analysis became everything. . . . Political and economic interests freed themselves from the international control of the Church, and from its cramping economic ethic.*[33]

It is true that Troeltsch was more interested in the differentiation of individuals than of societal spheres: nevertheless, the two are related. Certainly his remarks are

---

[33] Ernst Troeltsch, *The Social Teaching of the Christian Churches,* trans. Olive Wyon (New York: Harper Torchbooks, 1960), I, 376–377.

important in elaborating the simple distinction between church and sect by injecting a third type. Indeed, he felt that mysticism would be increasingly prominent among the middle classes of the twentieth century.

More direct support for our argument comes from R. H. Tawney. Earlier we noted his evidence that Protestant parishioners were neither as pliant nor as attentive as Weber seemed to assume. But, of course, he said much more as well. He is sometimes regarded as Weber's leading critic and as an advocate of the Marxian view that Protestantism was "caused" by capitalism itself. Actually, this puts Tawney's views far too strongly. He was highly sympathetic to Weber and regarded himself as less of an opponent and more of a clarifier. Tawney shied away from a polemic of his own; he was a man who was elegantly ambiguous on many counts, and his evocative metaphors were sometimes at cross-purposes in their total effect. And yet Tawney did suggest a thesis, one to which our own is in obvious debt:

> That economic transactions were one department of ethical conduct, and to be judged, like other parts of it, by spiritual criteria . . . such doctrines were still common ground to all sections of religious thought. It was precisely this whole conception of a social theory based ultimately on religion which was being discredited. While rival authorities were discussing the correct interpretation of economic ethics, the flank of both was turned by a powerful body of lay opinion, which argued that economics were one thing and ethics another.[34]

It is true that Tawney was less bold than we have been in assigning Protestantism a role in this process. At the same

---

[34] For an expression of Tawney's later sympathy and admiration for Weber, see the Preface to the 1937 edition of Tawney, *op. cit.*, pp. 3–9.

time, he concurred in assessing the results of the age generally.[35]

Of course, there is a Marxian reply even here. Joining once again their basic disagreement with Weber, Marxists may argue that it is ludicrous to think that any changes at all within the religious sphere will have a meaningful effect on the economy. After all, religion trades in ideas and values; the economy involves material conditions and social structure—and the latter are so dominant as to be immune from other influences. From Weber's perspective (and our own), this points out a crucial problem with Marxian theory generally: it *assumes* a differentiated society rather than regarding differentiation itself as a problematic process. Moreover, even the Marxian view of differentiation is distorted, for it is alloyed with an economic determinancy whereby the economy is protected from other forces all the while exercising an all-powerful force of its own. At least, this is true of the early Marx of the "Manifesto" and many subsequent Marxists, though it should be pointed out that later Marx and Engels retreated from the position somewhat as they witnessed the many variables at play in nineteenth-century German and French politics.[36]

But one can defend Weber without impugning the genius

---

[35] *Ibid.*, p. 155.

[36] The difference between the early and later Marx (and Engels) is even greater than that between the early and later Weber. But unfortunately Marx is still interpreted as if the *Communist Manifesto* was his ultimate product rather than a beginning polemic. Indeed, Marx's sociology only reached maturity when he began to reflect on factors conspiring against quick implementation of his polemic. At this point he was forced to analyze reality in more detail; hence the crucial importance of such contingencies as "class consciousness," "false consciousness," and relative versus absolute deprivation. It became clear that economic forces were indeed vulnerable to factors such as religion, at least as these factors operated through the actions of individuals in a complex societal web.

of Marx. The title of Weber's essay should be taken seriously in its reference to "the spirit" of capitalism. It is precisely this spirit that is at primary issue throughout his
work; he was only secondarily concerned with its material
and structural trappings. Of course, some Marxians may
reply that the spirit itself is unimportant and epiphenomenal; but this position is difficult to defend and, short of it,
at least a revised version of the Weberian thesis makes
sense. Protestantism was important to the ultimate rise of a
system of values conducive to rational capitalistic enterprise. Although it was probably more important for its
negative impact than its positive ethic, it nevertheless dem-
onstrates that the world of values is often crucial if we are
to understand the world of men. Weber is guilty as charged
of a host of historical inaccuracies and a thesis that is misleading in its broader import. Still, the thesis is worth
saving in altered form, and the fundamental theory behind
it continues to be both stimulating and relevant.

Postscript: A Leap to the Present

So far in this and the preceding chapter, we have
strayed considerably from what may be viewed as the
model of the proper sociology text. First, we have concen-
trated on the work of one man in particular—Max Weber.
Second, we have viewed Weber against the backdrop of the
chronological development of Christianity and encroached
upon the realm of the historian. It is apparent that this little
volume can ill-afford to follow either trend much further.
Somehow we must move quickly from Weber to a host of
more contemporary scholars and from Reformation Europe
to the present day.

Actually the concept of differentiation itself provides a
convenient conceptual bridge. First, one can argue that

what happened during the Reformation in Europe is happening similarly among contemporary developing nations. Traditional religion and traditional culture in general are being eclipsed by currents of political and economic modernism. Indeed, James S. Coleman has argued that Christianity's role with respect to native religion in Africa is similar to the role we have outlined for Protestantism with respect to European Catholicism.[37] As Protestantism broke the spell of Catholic dominance as an important prelude to autonomous capitalism, so has missionary Christianity broken the spell of indigenous tribal religion as a precursor to unfettered nationalism. From the missionaries' standpoint, the consequence was generally unintended. Nevertheless, once again sectarianism may lead to differentiation and to secularization, with its attendant joys and agonies.

Differentiation also continues to apply among the complex societies of the West. Certainly there has been further differentiation within the religious sphere itself. H. Richard Niebuhr's classic work *The Social Sources of Denominationalism*[38] makes it clear that after religion was fully exposed to such pressures as social class, regionalism, nationalism, and race, more divisiveness was sure to follow. In tracing the fragmentation of Protestantism from its inception to the twentieth-century United States, Niebuhr continued the work started by Troeltsch and, like him, had personal misgivings about the history recorded. To Niebuhr, the proliferation of denominations (for example, the rise of such groups as Methodists and Baptists, with the further differentiation of each into northern and southern, Negro and white wings) was a wound in the body of

---

[37] James S. Coleman, "Social Change and Religious Conflict," *The Journal of Social Issues*, 12 (1956), 44–56.

[38] H. Richard Niebuhr, *The Social Sources of Denominationalism* (New York: Holt, Rinehart and Winston, 1929).

Christ, an "ethical failure," and a blow to the possible
panacea for us all. It is on this point that debate has
ensued. Without questioning the fact of religious differentiation or denominationalism, Talcott Parsons has offered
a different view of the consequences.[39] Thus, in a complex
society, religion must be differentiated if it is to minister
meaningfully to the variegated needs of variegated groups.
Religious pluralism is important if religion is to remain vital
sociologically, if not theologically. Indeed, vitality has long
been associated with American religion in all of its differentiation more than with the more homogeneous and politically ordained Catholicism of parts of Europe and Latin
America. Ironically, the existence of an officially recognized
state religion may be related to less rather than more
religious fervor.

And yet this last statement may suggest too much. One
must distinguish between religious vitality with respect to
religious matters per se and religious vitality with respect to
secular issues in the wider society. It is quite possible to
have one without the other. As we have seen for the Reformation, one must examine not only differentiation within
the religious sphere itself but also differentiation between
the religious and all other societal domains.

In recent years, sociology has spawned a new evolutionism that avoids many of the foibles of the nineteenth-century evolutionists. The new version does not hold that all
change is "progress" or that societies can be invidiously
ranked on some value-laden scale of development. It does
not even assert that all societies must go through the same
substantive stages. The new evolutionists talk less about
substantive labels than about common analytic processes.
Key among these processes is the concept of differentiation

39 Talcott Parsons, *Structure and Process in Modern Societies* (New
York: Free Press, 1960), especially Chapter X.

itself. Thus, Robert Bellah has recently suggested that the history of Western religion can be analyzed as a process of steadily increasing differentiation between religion and other facets of society.[40] Bellah's larger thesis is obviously congruent with our own attempt to unravel the debate over effects of the Protestant Ethic. In general, we concur with Bellah in the broad sweep, but it is important to note some exceptions.

Rather than treat differentation as an inexorable and ever-mounting process, we would prefer to treat it as a variable that may or may not occur under varying circumstances. Moreover, it is important not to overlook the opposite process of dedifferentiation or the contraction of societal spheres into a unified package, whether bound coercively by a totalitarian political regime or tied informally by a collective societal response to an apparent threat. Both differentiation and dedifferentiation ebb and flow with the tides of history. Both can exist concurrently in the same society either in different locales or with respect to different aspects of society. Although Bellah is almost certainly correct in noting that religion has become highly differentiated from the rest of society in the twentieth-century United States, there are some fascinating exceptions.

Consider, for example, Liston Pope's study of the relations between the churches and the textile mills in Gastonia, North Carolina, in the late 1920s.[41] Here was a small

---

[40] Robert N. Bellah, "Religious Evolution," *American Sociological Review*, 29 (June 1964), 375–385. See also Talcott Parsons' broader statement of the evolution cum differentiation position, together with S. N. Eisenstadt's critique of the position, in the same issue with Bellah's article. Of course, the concept of differentiation has a noble history of its own that should not be disregarded. For an early statement, consider Robert MacIver, *Society* (New York: Holt, Rinehart and Winston, 1931).

[41] Liston Pope, *Millhands and Preachers*, 2nd. ed. (New Haven, Conn.: Yale University Press, 1965).

community unable to sustain a high degree of differentiation, especially in the midst of a mill strike that was instigated by outsiders who posed an external threat. The churches were forced to become involved in the economic crisis and to bow to the terms of the most powerful community force, the mill owners. In some situations, churches have a choice of either participating in wider issues at the expense of being compromised or maintaining their integrity at the cost of silence. But in Gastonia the local churches had no real alternative. Their economic and social dependency forced them to take the first option even though it meant opposing the positions taken by their statewide denominational conventions.

Gastonia is hardly typical, however, and Bellah, we believe, is *generally* correct in his diagnosis of the contemporary religious scene. The church is expected to minister to narrowly defined religious needs, but it neither exercises nor is accorded much influence in political or economic affairs.[42] As we shall see later, this differentiated autonomy is both a blessing and a curse. In any event, it provides a perspective from which to view the church as a deviant island in a secular sea. Of course, the church is not alone in its deviance. In a highly differentiated society, every institution is deviant to the extent that it distorts the larger system of values in pursuing its own special identity and its own narrowly defined set of goals. The plight of the individual in such a society is to seek adjustment by balancing his deviant commitments. But this may be a source of freedom as well. The church is only one possible commitment

---

[42] For a documentation of the church's loss of influence during the nineteenth and early twentieth centuries see Henry F. May, *Protestant Churches and Industrial America* (New York: Harper & Row, 1949); and Martin E. Marty, *The Infidel: Free Thought and American Religion* (New York: Meridian Books, 1961).

among many, and the individual has a choice of many institutions through which to provide meaning for his life. This
is precisely the sort of freedom that the rise in Protestantism
helped to provide; and although this is only one perspective
on the changing relations between religion and society, it
should provide boundaries for the more detailed discussion
of the contemporary scene that follows.

PART TWO

Perspectives on the Present and Future of Religion in the United States

IV

ASSESSING INDIVIDUAL RELIGIOSITY

This chapter marks a departure from its predecessors in Part One. There we used anthropology and history as a screen on which to project the conceptual unfolding of the sociology of religion. Here we shall begin to use newer as well as older concepts in seeking to understand the contemporary religious scene in the United States. The present chapter surveys a number of efforts to measure the religious attitudes and behavior of individuals. In the process, we shall extract various methodological and theoretical problems besetting the scientific analysis of religiosity. Next, Chapter V considers religion from an organizational rather than an individual perspective. No less than any other bureaucratically organized activity, the church must contend with intramural problems, and we shall offer a scheme for understanding such problems as they arise both out of and quite apart from religious doctrine itself. Chapter VI then investigates the relationships between religious organizations and the wider society. Whether one examines the church's role in providing integration and a sense of community or its role as an instrument of reform, the church's impact has undergone change in American society and, indeed, may be more problematic today than ever before. In sum, whereas Part One took up broad theoretical concerns against the backdrop of history, Part Two narrows these concerns to the present day. Still theoretical, our discussion nevertheless draws on more recent and empirical social scientific literature. Still seeking to generalize our views to religion in other societies—especially other complex societies—we shall largely confine our observations to religion in the United States as that which we know best.

Measures of Religiosity in Skeptical Review

An apocryphal story could be told about the naïve, upper-class investigator of recreational patterns who interviewed residents of slums. "How often do you play polo?" he asks. "Do you hunt foxes or play lawn tennis?" Learning that none of his respondents does any of these things, the researcher then concludes that slum residents engage in no recreation—or so the story goes.

Discovering how individuals express their religion—determining how "religious" various people are—can be a similar experience. Regardless of the notion of religion with which we begin, we can be much too naïve in our attempts to measure it. And just as the quest for accurate measurement is vital for the sociology of religion, so are errors of measurement and inference a plague to those who would understand religion in society. To see just how common such errors are, we begin with a review of pitfalls and prat-falls in assessing America's changing religiosity since the nineteenth century, a review revealing the confusion in measuring religiosity generally. Following sections take apart the notion of religiosity, discussing, in turn, matters of definition and conceptualization, the institutionalization of religious sentiments, and finally several recent typologies of religious expression.

Changing Patterns of Individual Religiosity in America?

Perhaps the most sobering experience for anyone drunk with the power of statistics on individual religious involvement is to examine the several arguments put forth concerning changes in American religion during the last century or so.[1] Consider, for example, the thesis of religious growth. Some argue that religion has undergone a steady increase in proportional adherence ever since the beginning of the nineteenth century; others argue the case for a "religious revival" in which adherence was seen to drop off between, say, 1840 and 1930, only to undergo a pronounced resurgence in the more recent past. There are, of course, meaningful differences between these two versions of the story of increasing religiosity. Still, the data are so poor that it is difficult to know not only which is correct but whether either is remotely close.

Surely the most commonly invoked statistics on behalf of

---

[1] For a greatly expanded treatment of the problems of assessing religious change, see N. J. Demerath III, "Trends and Anti-Trends in Patterns of Religious Change in America," in Wilbert E. Moore and Eleanor Bernert Sheldon (eds.), *Toward the Measurement of Social Change* (New York: Russell Sage Foundation, 1968).

proportional religious growth generally are the data on the changing percentage of *church members* in the population. For example, some 16 percent of the population were church members in 1850, but membership increased to 36 percent by 1900, to 47 percent by 1930, to 57 percent by 1950, and to 64 percent by 1965. Yet there are two fundamental flaws that bedevil any inference here. First, the statistics may simply be wrong. This is not the place to launch an extensive discussion of their methodological shortcomings, but several problems can be quickly listed. Thus, the U.S. Bureau of the Census has never included religion in any form in the regular census tallies, so these figures depend upon numbers supplied by the various denominations themselves to the National Council of Churches, serving as a central data collector. This practice has had several unhappy consequences. For one thing, not all denominations report their figures even today, and much of the increment over the last century comes from new groups reporting for the first time as the years go by. Even the groups that have always reported, however, have undergone changes in their definitions of "church members." Originally most Protestant groups reserved the label for those over thirteen years old, but Catholics and Jews included children as well. Gradually, however, Protestant groups have also begun to include children, thus enormously inflating the figures. There also are the various factors grouped under the general heading of mobility. Insofar as there has been an increase in vertical mobility in the social class system (and this is not easy to establish), this mobility has probably worked to increase formal membership counts, for, as we shall see later, high-status people tend to take out formal church membership more often than equally "devout" lower-class individuals. But certainly there has been a rise in geographical mobility as people increasingly shift their residence around the country. They also, therefore, engage in interparish, and sometimes interdenominational, mobility as a consequence. The problem here is one of increased multiple counting; that is, the mobile individual is quickly added to the rolls of his new congregation but not so quickly dropped from the tally of his previous parish. This duplication is partly a function of inefficient bookkeeping, but it also results from churches' reluctance to reduce their numbers, because their budgets and sometimes their prestige depend upon successful competition in the continuing quest for membership growth. To the extent that the quest has become more serious over time (for reasons to be indicated in Chapter V), the self-reported membership figures have been impugned.

There is another basic reason for suspicion concerning the membership statistics over time. Even if these statistics were beyond criticism, they would remain problematic in the interpretation. Certainly one should avoid the quick assumption that church members are always highly religious in their personal beliefs and activities or that nonmembers are otherwise irreligious. Membership in churches, like membership in virtually every other type of voluntary organization, is directly related to social class,[2] but there are other measures of religiosity that have negative relations with class, and one cannot help wondering whether high-status church membership is frequently a matter of form rather than substance. Ours is increasingly a society of joiners, and for many, church membership may mean little more than another membership in their roster of affiliations.

Much of the same reasoning can be applied to the next

---

[2] A good brief discussion of such relationships can be found in Michael Argyle, *Religious Behavior* (New York: Free Press, 1959). For a lengthier analysis, see N. J. Demerath III, *Social Class in American Protestantism* (Chicago: Rand McNally, 1965).

most prominent source of support for the thesis of religious growth: the changing rates of *church attendance.* Like membership, attendance also tends to be a high- rather than a low-status form of religious involvement, and its relations with other forms of religiosity ranging from beliefs to emotional feeling are similarly imperfect. It is true that the statistics of church attendance show a slight increase between 1939 and 1965, but the pattern is more complicated and perhaps no more reliable than that for church membership. Gallup poll results for national samples indicate that 41 percent claimed to have attended church during the week preceding the interview in 1939. This figure dropped to 36 percent in 1942, but thereafter climbed fairly steadily until 1958, when it stood at 49 percent, only to suffer a subsequent decline to 44 percent in 1965. Note that the percentage differences are small, not always consistent, and based upon sampling procedures that are by no means free from errors resulting in minor fluctuations. Moreover, research indicates that people are likely to inflate their reports of church attendance in response to an interviewer's question. In this connection, there may even be a "self-fulfilling prophecy" at work, for the phrase "religious revival" has taken on normative proportions and some respondents may feel obliged either to attend or to report attendance in order to feel comfortably conformist.

Of course, a number of indicators of religious involvement are similar to church attendance and church membership in various respects. Such measures as the number of activities participated in within the parish, Sunday school attendance, and financial contributions are all related to what could be termed the high-status "doing" dimension of religiosity. But there are other indicators reflecting the more emotional dimension of religious "feeling." As one might expect, it is much harder to tap this dimension empirically.

Indeed, one of the abiding ironies in research is that the most important aspects of a situation are often the most difficult to measure.

Let us take, for example, the question of religious belief. The data are certainly scanty for the past, and there is hardly an embarrassment of riches for the present. But consider the repeated findings from year to year that between 95 and 97 percent of national samples answer yes to the question "Do you believe in God?" What does this percentage mean? It may mean only that more than nine out of ten answer questions from strangers so as to avoid the stigma of a nonconformist, atheistic no. Surely there are various ways to believe in God and various definitions of God itself. For example, one study of a sample of university students found that 86 percent answered yes to the simple question of whether or not they believed in God, but when the group was later asked to pick one of five specific statements concerning God that came closest to their own conception, 46 percent chose statements that were agnostic or otherwise nonorthodox.[3] Moreover, even among those who

---

3 These data come from a study of that least reliable of all groups, introductory sociology students. See N. J. Demerath III and Richard Levinson, "On Baiting the Dissident Hook: The Methodology of Religious Belief," unpublished paper, University of Wisconsin, 1967. But note that even here the extent of religious doubt may be underestimated. Religious dissidence, even atheism itself, may be an instance of the "normatively deviant but statistically normal" in that many feel obliged to scoff publicly at disbelief even though they themselves are disbelievers in private. Certainly the study of religious belief poses methodological problems for the researcher seeking to penetrate beyond the respondent's public pose. Indeed, because the social context of almost any interview or questionnaire exerts biases in favor of a conforming religious orthodoxy, it may be necessary to use opposite biases in one's instrument to legitimate and facilitate an irreligious response where it is genuine. This goal is actually the more important burden of the above study. It explores several such countervailing biases and then asks the respondents

hold the same conception of God, there are sure to be differences in the extent of doubt and urgency that accompanies their beliefs.

Though coming from theologians rather than parishioners, the current "Death of God" movement reflects in the extreme the variation possible within the position of "believer." Analyzed admirably by Peter Berger,[4] the movement is chided in the following obituary parody, which appeared originally in the Methodist student magazine *motive:*

> ATLANTA, GA., *Nov. 9—God, creator of the universe, principal deity of the world's Jews, ultimate reality of Christians, and most eminent of all divinities, died late yesterday during major surgery undertaken to correct a massive diminishing influence. His exact age is not known, but close friends estimate that it greatly exceeded that of all other extant beings.*
>
> *The cause of death could not be immediately determined, but the deity's surgeon, Thomas J. J. Altizer, 38, of Emory University in Atlanta, indicated possible cardiac insufficiency. . . .*
>
> *In Johnson City, Texas, President Johnson was described by aides as "profoundly upset." He at once directed that all flags should be at half-staff until after the funeral. The First Lady and the two Presidential daughters, Luci and Lynda, were understood to have wept openly. Both houses of Congress met in Washington at noon today and promptly adjourned after passing a joint resolution expressing "grief and great respect for the departed spiritual leader." Senator Wayne Morse, Democrat*

---

themselves to evaluate the accuracy of their responses under each condition. It appears that the "dissident" bias is in fact more preferable than the "traditional" bias, though the latter has certainly been more common, if unacknowledged, in previous research.

4 Peter L. Berger, "A Sociological View of the Secularization of Theology," *Journal for the Scientific Study of Religion,* 6 (Spring 1967), 3–16.

of Oregon, objected on the grounds that the resolution violated the principle of separation of church and state, but he was overruled by Vice President Hubert Humphrey, who remarked that "this is not a time for partisan politics."

. . . Reaction from the world's great and from the man in the street was uniformly incredulous. "At least he's out of his misery," commented one housewife in an Elmira, N.Y., supermarket. "I can't believe it," said the Right Rev. Horace W. B. Donegan, Protestant Episcopal Bishop of New York. In Paris, President de Gaulle in a 30-second appearance on national television, proclaimed "God is dead! Long live the republic! Long live France!" News of the death was included in a one-sentence statement, without comment, on the 3rd page of Izvestia, official organ of the Soviet Government. The passing of God has not been disclosed to the 800 million Chinese who live behind the bamboo curtain.

Public reaction in this country was perhaps summed up by an elderly retired streetcar conductor in Passaic, N.J., who said: "I never met him, of course. Never even saw him. But from what I heard I guess he was a real nice fellow. Tops." From Independence, Mo., former President Harry S. Truman, who received the news in his Kansas City barbershop, said: "I'm always sorry to hear somebody is dead. It's a damn shame." In Gettysburg, Pa., former President Dwight D. Eisenhower released through a military aide the following statement: "Mrs. Eisenhower joins me in heart-felt sympathy to the family and many friends of the late God. He was, I always felt, a force for moral good in the universe. Those of us who were privileged to know him admired the probity of his character, the breadth of his compassion, the depth of his intellect. Generous almost to a fault, his many acts of kindness to America will never be forgotten. It is a very great loss indeed. He will be missed."

. . . Dr. Altizer, God's surgeon, in an exclusive interview with the Times, stated this morning that the death was "not unexpected." "He had been ailing for some time," Dr. Altizer said, "and lived much longer than most

of us thought possible." He noted that the death of God had, in fact, been prematurely announced in the last century by the famed German surgeon, Nietzsche. Nietzsche, who was insane the last 10 years of his life, may have confused "certain symptoms of morbidity in the aged patient with actual death, a mistake any busy surgeon will occasionally make." Dr. Altizer suggested, "God was an excellent patient, compliant, cheerful, alert. Every comfort modern science could provide was made available to him. He did not suffer—he just, as it were, slipped out of our grasp."[5]

Of course, such a satirical illustration of changing religious belief may be both seductive and spurious. As the obituary suggests, earlier eras have had their coroners of God, and it is not hard to find evidence of nonsalient beliefs and even disbelief itself in nineteenth-century America. Surely one must be wary of overinterpreting the phenomenon. For one thing, the phrase "death of God" is more spectacular than its substance warrants. It actually refers more to the death of one conception of God (an abstract, otherworldly "being" who is "out there" and hence little implicated in the social and ethical agonies of the present world) than to a death of God in a conventional atheistic sense. The movement puts a high premium on Jesus as a symbol for ethical action in this world. Far from calling for the demise of religion, it urges a revitalization. Moreover, for all of its press and attention, the movement remains a small minority. It by no means includes all theologians, let alone all clergymen or all parishioners. Many laity have been indignant at the thought that churchmen should think it; others have merely yawned at the doctrinal "happening."

Still, there is a good deal of doubt among parishioners, even though this is no necessary indication of any death of

---

[5] Anthony Towne, *motive*, February 1966, by permission. And by permission of Harper & Row, Publishers, Inc.

God in their minds. Table 1 (see page 128) from a recent study of a national sample by Charles Y. Glock and Rodney Stark,[6] lists the proportions of various denominations who had *no doubts* about the existence of God.

Unfortunately, there are no data comparable to these for nonchurch members (though one should not automatically conclude that nonmembers will have higher rates of doubt, because, as we have already indicated, church membership is far from a perfect predictor of other aspects of religiosity). Nor are good data available for earlier periods. Insofar as one is concerned with the question of *changing* beliefs, he must rely on approximations. What is worse but predictable, the approximations are themselves inconsistent. For example, consider the Gallup and Roper poll data on belief in life after death. Perhaps surprisingly these figures reveal that the percentage believing actually increased from 64 percent in 1936 to 76 percent in 1944, after which it declined insignificantly to 74 percent in 1961. Of course, one wonders what is meant by the ambiguous phrase "life after death." One can even speculate about the effect of the seemingly trivial fact that the 1936 poll was conducted in May, during the religious "off-season," whereas the 1944 and 1961 polls were administered in December and November, close to Christmas and Thanksgiving. Then, too, there are indications that the belief in an afterlife has actually declined among such special subgroups as scientists and college students.[7]

---

6 Charles Y. Glock and Rodney Stark, *Christian Beliefs and Anti-Semitism* (New York: Harper & Row, 1966), p. 190. For a more extensive analysis of this and related doctrinal issues in a sample of church members from the San Francisco Bay Area, see Glock and Stark, *Religion and Society in Tension* (Chicago: Rand McNally, 1965), especially Chapter 5.

7 For a more complete set of references to these and other belief data over time, see Demerath, "Trends and Anti-Trends," *op. cit.*

TABLE 1
Belief in God (National Sample)

Group[a]	*"I know God really exists and I have no doubts about it."*
Unitarian (9)	22%
Congregational (44)[b]	63
United Presbyterian (75)	67
Protestant Episcopal (56)	72
Methodist (217)	78
Presbyterian Church USA (40)	70
Disciples of Christ (42)[c]	73
American Lutheran bodies (146)[d]	70
TOTAL MODERATE PROTESTANTS (628)	72
Lutheran, Missouri Synod (45)	70
Evangelical and Reformed (28)[b]	71
American Baptist (91)	82
Southern Baptist (187)	93
Other Baptist bodies (90)	86
Sects (128)[e]	90
TOTAL CONSERVATIVE PROTESTANTS (569)	86
TOTAL PROTESTANTS (1,197)	79
TOTAL CATHOLICS (507)	85

[a] Figures in parentheses show the number of respondents on which percentages are based.

[b] The Congregational and the Evangelical and Reformed denominations merged several years ago to form a single body under the name of the United Church of Christ. However, because of the extreme contrasts in religious outlook between members of the two original bodies we have presented them here separately under their old names.

[c] Officially the Christian Church.

[d] Included here are the Lutheran Church in America and the American Lutheran Church. There were no important differences between members of these two bodies.

[e] Included in the category of sects were: Assemblies of God, Church of Christ, Church of God, Four Square Gospel, Free Methodist, Mennonite, Nazarene, Pentecostal, Salvation Army, Seventh Day Adventist,

Campbellite, Jehovah's Witnesses, Christian Missionary Alliance, Mission Covenant, and various tiny holiness bodies. Excluded were such groups as Christian Science, Unity, Divine Science, Theosophy, and Spiritualists, which most properly should be classified as cults for our analysis, but because only eleven persons in the sample claimed affiliation with bodies of this type, such a general category seemed futile. Also excluded were persons who claimed affiliation with the various Eastern Orthodox churches and one member of each of the major Asian faiths.

SOURCE: Charles Y. Glock and Rodney Stark, *Christian Beliefs and Anti-Semitism* (New York: Harper & Row, 1966), p. 190.

Although it is difficult to arrive at any firm quantitative assessment of the waxing and waning of particular religious beliefs over time, there is one bit of data that may serve as a more general projective test. George Gallup has recently cited the trend since 1957 in answer to the question "At the present time, do you think religion as a whole is increasing its influence on American life, or losing its influence?"[8] The percentage of national samples holding that religion was losing influence was 14 percent in 1957, but this figure rose to 31 percent by 1962 and to 57 percent by 1967. Gallup himself cited this as "one of the most dramatic shifts in surveys of American life," one that characterizes Catholics as well as Protestants, old as well as young, women as well as men, college graduates as well as the noneducated. Although there are certainly vagaries to prompt suspicion,[9] the finding does square with the general impression that

---

[8] George Gallup, American Institute of Public Opinion release, April 11, 1967.

[9] One such source of suspicion involves earlier data on the same point. Gallup cited only the trend since 1957, but if one goes to the massive compilation of public opinion data in Hadley Cantril, *Public Opinion, 1935–1946* (Princeton, N.J.: Princeton University Press, 1951), p. 742, one finds that as of January 1937 some 49.9 percent of a national sample questioned by Elmo Roper felt that religion was losing influence. Moreover, Gallup himself did a study in February 1939 that revealed that 34 percent felt that the "influence of religion in this community has decreased during the last few years." Apparently the 14 percent figure of 1957 was peculiarly low.

there has been a decline in the *saliency* of religious belief, if not a rise in the proportion of strict atheists or agnostics.

If this impression is accurate, it is worth relating to our earlier discussion of the "doing" aspects of religiosity. Let us assume that there was some increase in such things as church attendance, at least between 1940 and 1960—though this is a tenuous assumption and, using the same statistics, one must also cite a drop-off since 1960. In any event, how might a rise in "doing" be related to a decline in "feeling"? Actually, the combination is not as bizarre as it may seem. One can plausibly argue that the secularization of religious doctrine was a precondition for an increase in religious activity. Thus, before the churches could begin to host an upsurge in participation, they had to deemphasize old orthodoxies that were out of place and out of time. To the extent that the churches have been able to modernize their doctrine, they have begun to make their appeal on grounds that are sometimes more current, whether in an ethical, a political, or merely a social sense. Thus, we see once again that the general concept of "religiosity" must be specified very closely indeed. There is a very real sense in which religious activity is less and less related to traditional religious beliefs and sentiments. This trend is not a matter for such labels as "hypocrisy" and "prostitution." Instead, it is a fundamental commentary on the changing sociological character of the multifaceted religious experience. We now turn to a more analytic discussion of that experience.

The Search for a Conceptual Framework of Individual Religiosity

To a significant degree the difficulty in assessing individual religiosity rests with an issue encountered in Chapter I: do we regard religion by some predetermined attributes (what it *is*) or by its consequences (what it *does*)? In the first chapter a "consequence" in question was societal cohesion, a property of groups. Now, however, we are concerned about the logical role played by an *individual* property, the effects on persons of their being religious. This question is part of the issue concerning functionalism in the sociology of religion: are we to define religion in terms of its "essence" or in terms of its "function"? One's position on this issue greatly determines his ensuing discussion of how individuals express their religion.

Definitions of religion in the social science literature have also tended to state either what religion *is* or what it *does*. Sir Edward Tylor's famous definition that religion is belief in spiritual beings qualifies as the first kind.[10] So, too, does Joachim Wach's more elaborate definition that religion everywhere is characterized by three expressions: the theoretical, or system of beliefs (doctrine); the practical, or system of worship (cultus); and the sociological, or system of social relationships (communion).[11] The assumption of most Americans is that "religion" means "religious organization," and individual religiosity is therefore measured by persons' attachment to some church. Indeed, as one of our colleagues says, only half in jest, the presumption of this equation between religion and church is so strong that an American cannot be simply an atheist; he must be a Catholic atheist, a Protestant atheist, or a Jewish atheist. Even the ostensible antithesis of "religion" is meaningful to Americans only in the context of a religious organization.

But perhaps most social scientific definitions of religion deal with function or consequence rather than essence.

---

10 See Chapter I for a more extended analysis of Tylor's views and for indication that such definitions are far from idle matters in the sociology of religion.

11 Joachim Wach, *Sociology of Religion* (Chicago: University of Chicago Press, 1944), Chapter 2.

Sometimes these definitions do not specify what the consequence is, as in Alfred N. Whitehead's "what the individual
does with his own solitariness."[12] Sometimes a very general
consequence is stated, as in Erich Fromm's "any system of
thought and action shared by a group which gives the individual a frame of orientation and an object of devotion."[13]
And sometimes the consequence is quite specific, as in
Kingsley Davis' definition, reminiscent of Durkheim's, that
religion is what will "justify, rationalize and support the
sentiments that give cohesion to the society."[14]

Forced to choose between definitions of essence and consequence according to their theoretical merit, one would
have to nominate definitions of consequence. From Emile
Durkheim and Max Weber, through Georg Simmel and
Bronislaw Malinowski, down to Paul Tillich and Talcott
Parsons in our day (to name only some whose influence on
social science has been great), most seminal thought about
religion has occurred when religion is defined functionally
in terms of what it does for man. The monumental work of
Weber, reviewed in the previous chapters, was theoretically
productive because, in part, it raised a question of what
kind of theology was meaningful to what kind of people.
Freud, as we saw in his later work, came to the view that
culture has in it the capacity to frustrate people, and religion is one method of coping with frustration. Simmel
analyzed religion as if it were a "sedative for the turbulence
of the soul."[15] Tillich has introduced the term "ultimate

---

[12] Alfred N. Whitehead, *Religion in the Making* (New York: Macmillan, 1926), p. 16.

[13] Erich Fromm, *Psychoanalysis and Religion* (New Haven, Conn.:
Yale University Press, 1950), p. 21.

[14] Kingsley Davis, *Human Society* (New York: Macmillan, 1950), p.
519.

[15] Georg Simmel, *Sociology of Religion,* trans. Curt Rosenthal (New
York: Wisdom, 1959), p. 32.

concern" into social science literature, partly to suggest that whatever is a man's highest loyalty is his religion.[16] Even if definitions of consequence have the greatest potential theoretically, their empirical payoff has been considerably less, especially as empirical interest turns less toward total societies and historical eras and more toward individuals and narrower strata of populations. Problems of functional definitions of consequence are enormous. How, after all, are we to compare one man's ultimate concern with another's? By how ultimate that concern is? By the attention one gives to ultimate rather than trivial or penultimate concerns? If one man collects stamps in his own solitariness and another finds that mountain climbing quiets his soul's turbulence, do we then consider stamp collecting or mountain climbing to be religious? Even assuming that the conceptual matters were resolved, the technical problems remain difficult. For example, how is "resolved frustration" or a "sedated soul" to be measured? No doubt, most people would grant that the problem is different from measuring the effects of bicarbonate of soda on the stomach's turbulence, but most people would probably disagree on *how* it is different.

Nevertheless, classifications have been attempted, some with interesting and valuable results. In his Gifford Lectures at the turn of the century, for example, William James identified two functional types of religious experience: that of the "healthy-minded" and that of the "sick soul."[17] The healthy-minded, sometimes called the once-born, are optimistic, living more "with flowers and birds and all enchanting innocencies than with dark human passions."[18] Such

---

16 Paul Tillich, *Dynamics of Faith* (New York: Harper & Row, 1957).
17 William James, *The Varieties of Religious Experience* (London: Longmans, Green, and Co., 1902.)
18 *Ibid.*, p. 77.

people, James asserted, have tendencies to conceive of God as an animating spirit, as a resource to be tapped, or as a "principle" with which to be in harmony. Theological systems congenial to the healthy-minded range from mind-cure movements to less radical, but also optimistic, Protestant incorporations of evolutionalism and progress. The situation for those with sick souls is different, for the "twice-born" see evil as the very essence of the universe. From Stoicism to pessimistic Protestantism, theologies congenial to the sick soul are rooted in notions of failure, humiliation, and sin. If one's original state is evil, then one must be born again to make life tolerable.

These two styles of religious experience, it should be noted, are for James characterizations of the "religious constitution"; they describe two kinds of *appetite,* not necessarily two kinds of food. If, therefore, one follows by extrapolation what happens when the appetite is fulfilled, one might observe a phenomenon made much of by other commentators on the religious experience—that religion motivates, "enables," or supplies the believer's enthusiasm for acting out his obligations. He has, to use Tillich's phrase, "the courage to be."[19] Faith, therefore (in this special sense of "faith enough in order to . . .") is the consequence of "being religious"; religion, correlatively, is that which supplies faith.

Looked at in this fashion, the religiosity of individuals may be investigated from at least two standpoints. One of these is used by Tillich when he discusses existential situations creating anxieties that challenge men and that therefore tend to elicit religious or "faith-fulfilling" responses. Just as epochs may be classified by which of three anxieties

---

[19] Paul Tillich, *The Courage To Be* (New Haven, Conn.: Yale University Press, 1952).

(ontic, spiritual, moral) predominates,[20] so also may individuals be seen as differing in personality, circumstance, opportunity, and so forth, and thus differing as well in "type" of religion found congenial. The fact is, however, that societies more often than strata are analyzed this way, and strata more often than individuals.[21]

A second standpoint from which a functional analysis of religiosity may be carried out is even less common—the standpoint that sees consequential "faith" or the "courage to be" as a variable and attempts to classify individuals by their *degree* of faith. One provisional but very interesting effort in this direction is Samuel Z. Klausner's research. Looking at both product and producing conditions, Klausner investigates very seriously the idea that religion has the function of enabling action in the face of anxiety. He therefore analyzes worship as a means of achieving faith, and he sees faith as a capacity to act.[22] Suggestions are given for assessing the worship process and its impact.

More examples could be given, but the point is already clear—that without theoretical precision and empirical

---

20 *Ibid.*, especially pp. 57–63.

21 See, however, a first step in Glock and Stark's Chapter 3, "A Taxonomy of Religious Experience," in *Religion and Society in Tension, op. cit.* The point above is nicely illustrated in Eric Hoffer's little classic *The True Believer* (New York: Harper & Row, 1951), where, in the Preface, he stated, "Though there are obvious differences between the fanatical Christian, the fanatical Mohammedan, the fanatical nationalist, the fanatical Communist and the fanatical Nazi, it is yet true that the fanaticism which animates them may be viewed and treated as one." However, though his Chapter 13 provides a number of suggestions about recognizing individual differences in fanaticism, the bulk of the analysis is of fanatic strata, not individuals.

22 See Samuel Z. Klausner, "Worship," a paper of the Bureau of Applied Social Research, Columbia University, 1959, and "The Social Psychology of Courage," *Review of Religious Research*, 3 (Fall 1961), 63–72.

measure, most of the functional approach to individual expressions of religion remains ambiguous. Frequently exciting and conducive to insights,[23] this approach is nevertheless far overshadowed in research into religiosity by the other approach—where religion is defined by what it *is* and persons are classified by how much of "it" they exhibit. For conceptual and technical reasons, almost all modern, empirical sociological comparisons of individual religious expressions start with some arbitrary conception of religious identification. Sometimes the arbitrariness may be minimal, as when identification as Catholic, Protestant, Jew, or "Other," in contrast to "No Religion," is used to locate the "religious" in America. Other times the arbitrariness is greater, as when a nineteenth-century, evangelical, Protestant, orthodox theology is used as a foil against which to measure persons' religiosity. It is easy to criticize these efforts as naïve and inadequate when their purported objective is to measure the extent of an individual's investment in the religious sphere. Before such charges are leveled, however, some attention to the underlying premise of the efforts is worthwhile. For it turns out that at least some theoretical justification exists for these endeavors, and our attention to this justification will uncover another issue in the area of individuals and their religion.

The Institutionalization of Individual Religious Sentiments

Much of the preceding section concerning definitions of religion is analogous to our earlier discussion of Tylor, Müller, and Freud in the primitive materials tradition (Chapter I). In both cases there is a tendency to treat

---

23 For example, the growing literature on the similarity between religion and psychiatry, as alternative "enablers" of action. This similarity, incidentally, was the source of Klausner's work cited here.

religion on a solely individual basis. Also in both cases there seems to be a need for the sort of sociological corrective that Durkheim provided in the first instance. Clearly individual religion does not occur in a social vacuum; measurements of individual religion should reflect the institutional setting in which that religion is most generally conceived and acted out. In fact, this is precisely the difference between the relatively nonsociological treatments of religion that we have just reviewed and the manifestly sociological treatments that are still to come. Whereas the former definitions tend to neglect or deemphasize the institutional setting, the latter, more empirical, treatments seek to take it into account. It is true that the accounting is often superficial and even opportunistic (because, after all, it is easier to ascertain an institutional identification than to probe the depths of the individual psyche). It is even true that many of these efforts go too far in the institutional direction, thus overemphasizing the impress of the "church" and giving short shrift to other factors. Still, the institutionalization of individual religious sentiment is undeniably crucial. Let us pause here to examine how it comes about and what accounts for its importance to those who would assess individual religion itself.

Of course, earlier chapters have already alluded to the institutionalization of religion from a variety of perspectives. Max Weber's treatment is most prominent, using such concepts as charisma and authority, theodicy, and the transition from sect to church. Yet Weber's theory tends to assume some form of religious institution in the first place, even if only a small and struggling sect. His analysis is largely from the perspective of an organization and its leaders rather than from the view of the individual adherent. The following discussion treats institutionalization precisely from the perspective of the individual adherent.

Without postulating any Freud-like vision of the "first believer," let us examine why a religion might change from the private sentiments of a "founder" to *the* religion of an entire society. What is it about religious sentiments that seems to produce some form of institutionalization if only to satisfy the individual believer himself?

One clue to such matters comes from a psychologist rather than a sociologist: Leon Festinger and his theory of cognitive dissonance.[24] Religious sentiments, because they are both nonempirical and important to their holders, cause those who hold them to seek out others who, by being "converted" to similar sentiments, thereby support and convince further the originators of the sentiments. Prophets, according to the theory, are not likely to remain recluses but will instead spread their message to others who, in turn, will be motivated to convert still others. The missionary impulse, then, is built into any religious movement, even though geographic and theological or other cultural factors may account for variations in the degree to which religious movements actually conduct missionary enterprises.

An imperiousness in spreading the message is not the only outcome for those who have already accepted the message; in addition, they are led to express *to each other* their common religious sentiments. The problem of reinforcement is a continuing one, in other words, and an organization for mutual reinforcement through ceremony, worship, and elaboration on the original theory is likely to arise.

---

[24] As set forth in Leon Festinger, "A Theory of Social Comparison Processes," *Human Relations,* 7 (1954), 117–140, and *A Theory of Cognitive Dissonance* (New York: Harper & Row, 1957). A specifically religious application of Festinger's theory is found in Leon Festinger, Henry W. Riecken, Jr., and Stanley Schachter, *When Prophecy Fails* (New York: Harper Torchbooks, 1965), a study considered in some detail in Chapter V.

This organization may, of course, take many forms, and it may—indeed very likely will—serve other purposes as well. At times of grief or good fortune, participants' activities and thoughts may be channeled into institutionalized forms so that not only are the immediate problems assuaged but so also is the theological superstructure reestablished and reanimated. During puberty rites in primitive tribes or surrounding the religious training of youth in the Sunday schools of modern societies, in addition to the ostensible transmission of knowledge to religious neophytes there is the (perhaps unintended) reinforcement in others of the authenticity of what is being transmitted. The sermon, the communion rite, the regular evening prayer, the ceremony that follows the planting of seeds—all serve to remind participants that the theological basis of what they do is real and believed in not only by themselves but by others also.

Other reasons can be adduced to help explain why religious sentiments tend to become institutionalized. Tillich emphasized the role of language, saying that "the act of faith, like every act in man's spiritual life, is dependent on language and therefore on community."[25] Even if one chose to remain religiously aloof, in other words, there is the temptation to use the community resource of language to express one's religion. Klausner referred to an even more basic proposition about social life. [All men are concerned that their fellows are motivated to live up to expectations; and therefore something like religious worship, as a potential source of motivation, is encouraged as a group act.[26]

---

[25] Tillich, *Dynamics of Faith, op. cit.*, pp. 23–24.

[26] For example, ". . . society has an interest in courage. . . . [T]herefore . . . social institutions develop means to assure individual achievement of courage or faith. This is a central function of the worship role in religious institutions." Klausner, *op. cit.*, p. 67.

It might be said that, in this context, the accuracy of these explanations is not so important as the seeming generalization initiating them: religious sentiments, once they appear in a society, have the potential of becoming institutionalized. How successful this institutionalizing process will be is another question, for as we saw in Chapter II, theological and structural factors intersect, producing sometimes sects, sometimes churches, sometimes variants or nothing at all. The point here is not that *any* system of religious sentiments will become established but rather that *some* one or more will tend to do so. It is not surprising, then, to find considerable similarity in the religious expressions of fellow members of a society.[27]

Thus, we might reasonably expect religion, conceived even in functional terms, to be expressed in more or less regularized fashion. Those for whom religion is more salient will manifest the salience in ways that are widely recognized as religious. Some persons would no doubt belie the assumption, either by expressing their salient religion in unorthodox ways or by expressing in orthodox ways various nonreligious concerns. But granting the imperfect correlation, we can at least see a basis in theory for using arbitrary, institutionalized aspects of religion in efforts to measure individual religious expressions.

Some of the more common of these aspects—church membership, church attendance, belief orthodoxy—have already been mentioned in the chapter's first section, concerning empirical assessments of religious change in America. These measures are used to buttress such statements as "women are more religious than men," "older people and

---

[27] It is in this sense that Simmel, *op. cit.*, p. 11, refers to religion as "the objectified world of faith."

callow youth are more religious than young adults," "Orthodox Jews are more religious than Conservative or Reform Jews," and "Ireland is a more religious society than Italy."[28] But our earlier section also mentioned difficulties and ambiguities of measurement and interpretation. [Some of these indicators refer to church behavior and the "doing" aspect of religiosity, whereas others relate to personal religious consequences and the "feeling" dimension of religion.] Some are fraught with bias in the measurement itself, but others are too vague to be relied upon for precise inferences. Some may be more accessible to the analyst than they are important to the adherent, but others may have the reverse characteristics. [Finally, some are positively related to such factors as social class, but others bear negative relationships even for the same group of church members.]

Two quite different reasons for never relying on a single measure or indicator to tap any phenomenon as complex as "individual religiosity" are thus suggested. In the first place, the possibility of bias in any one measure is too great to be ignored without counterbalancing measures; in the second place, precisely because of the phenomenon's complexity, several indicators should be used to tap its several dimensions. Let us now review some recent attempts to classify a number of dimensions with their various indicators into a single overall scheme. All these reflect an appreciation of the institutionalized aspects of individual religion, but none has reached the point of providing a panacea for our theoretical and empirical woes.

---

28 For example, a good summary of the "religious map" of the United States using church attendance as an indicator is Bernard Lazerwitz, "Religion and Social Structure in the United States," in Louis Schneider (ed.), *Religion, Culture and Society* (New York: Wiley, 1964), pp. 426–439.

Some Recent Classifications and Typologies of Individual Religiosity

℥ One of the first multidimensional schemes to be used in empirically sorting out various categories of individual religiosity was that of Joseph Fichter in his study of Catholic parishioners in a large Southern city.[29] Fichter's scheme is called a typology in that he not only identified the ingredient dimensions but gave names to the intersections of these dimensions, names that correspond to types of individuals. Thus, he identifies four kinds of Catholic. Beginning with a territorial population defined as Catholic because of baptism or ethnic origin, Fichter then classified these persons as *nuclear, modal, marginal,* or *dormant,* depending upon participation in prescribed rituals (mass, confession, parochial education for their children), participation in the organizations of the church, and degree of interest (as expressed in interviews) in the parish. In the Southern city he investigated, some 39 percent were found to be *dormant,* that is, doing nothing more than acknowledging they are Catholic, and perhaps not even that. Another 13 percent were called *marginal* because, though they did not sufficiently meet all the prescribed requirements, they met some. The remaining 48 percent met all the minimum requirements; this group was subdivided into the few *nuclear* parishioners (7 percent) and the more usual *modal* type (41 percent).

The conceptual clarity of Fichter's procedure has great merit, utilizing as it does an image of successive concentric

---

[29] Joseph H. Fichter, S.J., *Southern Parish* (Chicago: University of Chicago Press, 1951). See also his "The Marginal Catholic, An Institutional Approach," *Social Forces,* 32 (December 1953), 167–173, and *Social Relations in the Urban Parish* (Chicago: University of Chicago Press, 1954), pp. 7–79.

rings extending from a church center. Of course, Catholics are more explicit than many religious groups with regard to a church center and a core of precise prescriptions. Nevertheless, Fichter's typology has been used to describe other faiths, the practice being to make all dividing lines arbitrary, not just the boundary between nuclear and modal, as in the case with Catholics. As an illustration, Charles Glock, Benjamin Ringer, and Earl Babbie adapted Fichter's typology to a study of parishioners in the Episcopal church and found, for example, that unmarried or childless persons are *relatively* more involved in the church.[30] The interpretation they give is that the church provides for these people what is available for others in family life. This approach is an example of how individual "functions" of religiosity may be investigated when religiosity is measured this way. But note that, even though several indicators of religious participation are used, there is still a tendency in these studies ultimately to lump them together into a single scale of overall religiosity. Thus, the researchers elected not to take advantage of the more explicitly multidimensional possibilities of their measurements. Instead, they returned to the notion that religion is expressed to various degrees along a single institutionalized path.

A modification of this single-path assumption occurs in Russell Dynes' research on religious attitudes of a sample of Columbus, Ohio, adult Protestants.[31] Borrowing the distinction between churches and sects, Dynes constructed a scale of twenty-four items reflecting *either* a churchlike re-

---

[30] Charles Y. Glock, Benjamin B. Ringer, and Earl R. Babbie, *To Comfort and to Challenge* (Berkeley: University of California Press, 1967), Chapter 3.

[31] Russell Dynes, "Church-Sect Typology and Socio-Economic Status," *American Sociological Review*, 20 (October 1955), 555–560.

ligious orientation *or* a sectlike religious orientation. He discovered, then, that persons of higher socioeconomic status, even in the same denomination, were more likely to have a churchlike orientation. Dynes used a mixture of items (for example, "Heaven and Hell are very real to me" and "I think that we should emphasize education in religion and not conversion"), so it is incorrect to think of his classification as a distinction in religious beliefs alone. The importance of the research lies in its demonstrating how *alternative* institutionalized ways for expressing religion are in fact variously expressed by different sectors of a population. Persons may be equally, though differently, involved religiously.[32]

An elaborate alternative scheme for measuring this multifaceted religious involvement is found in Gerhard Lenski's *The Religious Factor*.[33] The focus of that research was the effects on daily life of religious "commitment," and Lenski sought several ways in which commitment might be expressed. He arrived at four, which he calls *associational* involvement, *communal* involvement, *doctrinal* orthodoxy, and *devotionalism*. The first two are behavioral in nature (how often church is attended and whether one's spouse and close friends are also members of one's socioreligious group), and the second two are less behavioral than "mental" (one being assent to the doctrines of one's church, the other being the frequency of private prayer or "communion" with God). Thus, it is possible to be religious in one way without being religious in other ways, and the data show that indeed this is the frequent pattern. To know that someone is associationally involved, for example, is not to know

---

[32] This issue is treated more extensively in Demerath, *Social Class in American Protestantism, op. cit.*, especially Chapter VIII.

[33] Gerhard Lenski, *The Religious Factor* (Garden City, N.Y.: Doubleday, 1961).

whether he is communally involved; orthodoxy and devotionalism are likewise only mildly related. One still might conceive of the "nuclear" parishioner, therefore, as the person who scores high on all four dimensions, but all others could not be placed in successive rings around a nucleus; rather, the image is now multidimensional, with persons variously located in the four-dimensional space.

But Lenski's monograph only begins with these categories. Its more important concern is to examine empirically the consequences of being religious in one or more of the four ways, a concern that returns us to our earlier distinction between definitions of essence and function. Perhaps it is worth dwelling a bit on the way in which such consequences are teased out.

Results from a Recent Classification Scheme

℣ Consider the findings on the relation between various aspects of religious involvement and political party preference. The data defy any simple summary. For example, among Catholics, preference for the Republican party is associated with (1) high associational involvement, (2) low communal involvement, and (3) high orthodoxy; but (4) devotionalism is unrelated to party preference.[34] Among Protestants, on the other hand, communal involvement is not related to party preference, and the relation with high orthodoxy is attenuated. Finally, note that some

---

[34] *Ibid.*, pp. 81–87. In this connection, see Benton Johnson's "Ascetic Protestantism and Political Preference," *Public Opinion Quarterly,* 26 (Spring 1962), 35–46, and "Theology and the Position of Pastors on Public Issues," *American Sociological Review,* 32 (June 1967), 433–442. Without arguing that theological persuasion *causes* party proclivity, Johnson's studies of Oregonians reveal that fundamentalists are more likely to vote Republican (despite their low status) and that modernists are more likely to vote Democratic (despite their generally higher socioeconomic status).

of these relationships are stronger among middle-class adherents, while others are greater among working-class adherents within both religious groups.

Lenski went on to analyze the consequences of different forms and degrees of religiosity in such areas as education, family life, and economic affairs. Indeed, this last category seems to revive the ghost of Weber and his earlier concern for Protestant-Catholic differences with respect to the "spirit of capitalism." A host of relevant findings are presented, but again they are not amenable to a broad summary in the Weberian tradition. For example, with social class held roughly constant, white Protestants are somewhat more likely than white Catholics to put a positive evaluation on work, and yet there is no significant difference between Protestants and Catholics with respect to economic aspiration and ambition. Moreover, the relationships with specific types of involvement are once again inconsistent. Church attendance is related to economic views, but surprisingly the degree of doctrinal orthodoxy is not.[35] Is there, in all these findings, a confirmation of Weber's thesis regarding the impact of a Protestant ethic on a capitalistic spirit? It clearly depends on how the data are interpreted. For one thing, Weber himself predicted a decline in the saliency of religious differences with respect to economic phenomena, as we saw in Chapter III. For another, Lenski's findings are often at odds with each other, and indeed they crumble at particularly strategic points, that is, with respect to economic aspirations and the effect of theological orthodoxy. Finally, there is a range of methodological considerations that must be confronted. Lenski's sample is precariously small for some of his more detailed analyses; it is also a sample of Detroit residents only. This last point is especially

---

[35] Lenski, *op. cit.*, pp. 158, 165, 182, 185.

important, because Lenski did not control for ethnicity, and Detroit Catholics are heavily Polish—which means that they may be more traditional, more ethnic, and hence less acculturated to American value patterns than are American Catholics generally. There are also major differences among the Protestant groups. Although Lenski distinguished throughout between white and Negro Protestants, there are denominational differences among white Protestants themselves. Finally, insofar as Lenski demonstrated that religious differences may be more important than social class differences in predicting economic, educational, family, and political behavior, there is room for skepticism here as well. He made the last point in a table that compares religious and class differences on some thirty-five items; he takes the respective mean differences on all thirty-five and finds that the mean is larger for religion than for class.[36] Note, however, that the cards are stacked. The mean religious difference is inflated by five items on such traditional points of religious debate as gambling, birth control, drinking, Sunday business, and divorce. If these five items are eliminated from the list, class is clearly the more important predictor of the remaining thirty items. Still, the larger point here is strongly in Lenski's favor. No work is without flaw, and *The Religious Factor* is a landmark effort to explore religious differences in terms of their consequences, an approach that this chapter has stressed from the beginning.

Including Consequences in the Measure of Religiosity

A recent variation in the multidimensional approach comes full circle and incorporates the "individual functions" as a dimension in its own right. Marking a

---

[36] *Ibid.*, pp. 293–294.

change from his study with Ringer and Babbie cited earlier in its single-path assumption, Charles Glock has identified five ways in which an individual may be religious.[37] One of these—the *ritualistic*—is most familiar in that it includes such common indicators as church attendance, practice of worship, and prayer. The *intellectual* dimension, a second way to be religious, is the degree to which a person is "informed and knowledgeable about the basic tenets of his faith and its sacred scriptures."[38] Related to the second dimension is a third—the *ideological,* or the degree to which religious beliefs are held with conviction. The fourth —the *experiential*—is a continuum reflecting emotional contact with or knowledge of the supernatural; "religious feeling" might be an adequate synonym here. The fifth dimension—the *consequential*—completes the scheme. Through the fifth dimension, "individual functions" are brought into the conceptualization of religiosity, for, by investigating consequences as part of commitment, one is in a position to assess how religion operates in individuals.

It is important to realize that developing dimensions of religion can be merely a taxonomic exercise, however. Finer

---

[37] See Glock and Stark, *Religion and Society in Tension, op. cit.,* Chapter 4. This dimensionalization has spawned a good deal of empirical research into the relationships that it deems problematic. Since both of us were students of Glock, it is understandable that we have been a part of the tradition. Thus, Demerath, *Social Class in American Protestantism, op. cit.,* argued that each of Glock's dimensions can be further divided into churchlike and sectlike modes of expression and that these are respectively high-status and low-status tendencies even within the same parish. And Phillip E. Hammond, "Contemporary Protestant Ideology: A Typology of Church Images," *Review of Religious Research,* 2 (Spring 1961), 161–169, investigated the relationship between the ideological and ritualistic dimensions. See also the work of another of Glock's students, Yoshio Fukuyama, "The Major Dimensions of Church Membership," *Review of Religious Research,* 2 (Spring 1961), 154–161.

[38] Glock and Stark, *Religion and Society in Tension, op. cit.,* p. 20.

and finer conceptual distinctions can be drawn for any phenomenon, but the justification of such activity lies in its demonstrated utility for uncovering relationships and thus increasing understanding. Lenski's work, we saw above, has this virtue. A similar endeavor, though more narrowly defined, is illustrated by Snell Putney and Russell Middleton's investigation of the ideological dimension.[39] They took this one dimension and asked whether *it* might be broken down into four subdimensions, which they call orthodoxy, fanaticism, importance, and ambivalence. Reasoning that a person could be high on one or more subdimensions but low on others (for example, an agnostic with missionary zeal would be low in orthodoxy but high in fanaticism), they found very little difference between the four subdimensions and the other factors they examined. That is to say, in the context at least of their research questions, the dimension of ideology seems to be a single dimension. In other contexts, of course, quite the contrary may be discovered, which simply says again that reality acts always to refine theory.

Surely such refinement is needed with respect to Glock and Stark's experiential dimension, one that was not explicit in past formulations such as Fichter's or Lenski's. Scholars have long investigated the religious "experience," it is true, but typically not as a variable. The concern generally has been with conversion, mysticism, or whatever, as discrete happenings rather than as an underlying dimension in the religious personality. An interesting example of this non-variable approach was found when W. Seward Salisbury asked 1,008 persons to respond to the question "When do you feel most religious?"[40] On the basis of their answers, he

[39] Snell Putney and Russell Middleton, "Dimensions and Correlates of Religious Ideologies," *Social Forces*, 39 (May 1961), 285–290.

[40] W. S. Salisbury, *Religion in American Culture* (Homewood, Ill.: Dorsey, 1964), pp. 56–67.

identified six situations in which the religious experience seems to arise, in the following order of frequency: (1) during the course of rituals, (2) during meditation, (3) under the influence of a charismatic leader, (4) in a "nature" setting, (5) at a time of crisis, and (6) in the family context. Catholics, Protestants, Jews, and nonbelievers were noted as differing both in the frequency with which they felt religious and the context in which such feelings occurred. The possibility of converting such a procedure into an investigation of degree of religious experience is obvious. Indeed, Glock and Stark, after developing their taxonomy of religious experience, argued that the types they identify

> may be . . . ordered on the basis of complexity, intimacy of the inter-actor relationship, frequency, . . . and variation in the degree to which they are encouraged or discouraged by both religious and secular norms. Furthermore, we have suggested that this order represents a developmental model and that persons pass from the less complex to the more complex during the career of their religious encounters.[41]

Whereas Glock and Stark's experiential dimension represents a small step away from tradition, however, their fifth dimension—the consequential—represents a huge departure; to include consequences for personal behavior as part of the religious phenomenon itself is to resume the functional discussions that have, as we said earlier, contributed most to the theory of religious behavior.

Let us be clear about what is—and is not—being said in this context. When *group* consequences or functions are at issue, the theoretical debate proceeds with only the usual misunderstandings. The religious status of classical civiliza-

---

[41] Glock and Stark, *Religion and Society in Tension, op. cit.*, p. 64. Some demonstration of the variable is given in their Chapter 8.

tions, for example, is analyzed from a perspective of their vitality as societies, their "failure of nerve," or their pursuit of ever-expanding humanitarian goals. Modern nations are discussed in terms of their sense of destiny and ultimate aims. The cohesion or integration of groups, in other words, is frequently seen as an intimate part of their "religiousness."

In social research, however, the "integrated personality" or the "courage to be" or the "humanitarianism" of individual persons has not been conceived of as an indication of religiosity. Instead, when such matters have been treated, they have been viewed either as separate phenomena or as possible consequences of being (or not being) religious. There is understandable reason for this treatment, because most efforts to demonstrate the moral effects on daily behavior of religion (narrowly defined) have failed.[42] Hugh Hartshorne and Mark A. May's classic finding that, whereas children's moral judgments correlate with their parents' at .55, the correlation with their Sunday school teachers' is .002,[43] is only one example. The religious orthodoxy of prison populations is another phenomenon that delights the cynic—and perhaps others.

The question, however, is not simply what *is* or *is not* religion. What seems fairly clear is, first, that religion is expressed in various ways, and these various ways do not operate in the same fashion. Second, the *kinds* of questions the sociological tradition has asked—questions at the level of society, community, or group—have rarely been asked at the level of the individual. How, for instance, does one take

---

42 Thus, making Lenski, *op. cit.*, one of the exceptions.

43 Hugh Hartshorne and Mark A. May, *Studies in Deceit* (New York: Macmillan, 1928). See also W. S. Salisbury, "Religiosity, Regional Subculture, and Social Behavior," *Journal for the Scientific Study of Religion*, 2 (Fall 1962), 94–101.

Durkheim's notion—that society marks off a sacred sphere, surrounds it with beliefs and rites, and thereby creates a device for maintaining the moral standards of the society—and translate it into an investigation of individual behavior, using the far more sophisticated techniques available at that level? The answer, of course, is that one cannot without reconceptualizing what religion is for individuals.

In modern societies only churches (and mosques, temples, synagogues, and so forth) are typically considered religious organizations, and only the ideologies developed and promulgated there are considered religious ideologies. When the consequential dimension is added to the portrait of individual religiosity, however, the sociology of religion is in a position to broaden its concerns. If it is discovered, for example, that political ideologies and political behavior function as religious ideologies and behavior for some individuals, then cannot political parties be analyzed as if they are, in some sense, religious organizations? Roger Caillois demonstrated the great conceptual similarity between many aspects of play or games and religion.[44] Might not the sociology of religion, then, profit from investigations of recreational activities viewed as religious activities?[45]

---

[44] Roger Caillois, *Man, Play and Games*, trans. Meyer Barash (New York: Free Press, 1961). Referring to mimicry of or identification with entertainment stars, for example, Caillois says, "The majority have only this illusion to give them diversion, to distract them from a dull, monotonous, and tiresome existence. . . . A continuous osmosis exists between these seasonal divinities and their multitude of admirers (p. 122). See also N. J. Demerath III and Victor Thiessen, "On Spitting Against the Wind: Organizational Precariousness and American Irreligion," *American Journal of Sociology*, 71 (May 1966), 674–687, where an "irreligious" organization is analyzed from a point of view commonly used to analyze "religious" organizations.

[45] One effort in the direction of this last example is Samuel Z. Klausner, "Worship and the Dangerous Life: A Study of Church Attendance Among Sport Parachutists," a report of the Bureau of Social Science Research, Inc., 1965.

These suggestions may be deemed unorthodox, and indeed they are. But the questions raised by the earliest sociologists of religion show little hope of modern-day pursuit until the horizons of modern research into religious behavior are broadened. Edward Shils stated the case this way:

> ✗   . . . *the agenda of sociological theory must find a place for religion. I do not mean the study of ecclesiastical institutions, or of the influence of beliefs about God's intentions on daily conduct, of church attendance, or attitudes towards priests. These are all interesting subjects. . . . [But] What I have in mind is a much more elusive and much more fundamental matter . . . the ways in which man's need for being in contact with sacred or charismatic things manifests itself in politics, in the legal system, in education and learning, as well as in the churches. Both Durkheim and Max Weber had a wonderful sense of this phenomenon, but this aspect of their understanding of society has not been taken up. The time is now ripe.*[46]

The functional approach, which, as we noted earlier in this chapter, has been used most often in societal-level investigations, should also appear in inquiries of individual religious expressions. With the inclusion of the consequential dimension as a component of religiosity, this approach becomes a possibility. If, to restate a point made above, faith or courage is one of the functional theorists' explanations for the appearance of religion in human society, then research into individual expressions of religion should provide a test of the theory.

---

[46] Edward Shils, "The Calling of Sociology," in Talcott Parsons, *et al.* (eds.), *Theories of Society* (New York: Free Press, 1961), II, 1445.

Summary

℞ This chapter has been more of a critique and a chart-ing of pitfalls than a celebration of current knowledge concerning individual religiosity. And yet the situation is not wholly discouraging. Even the relatively few studies of individual religiosity cited in this chapter are enough to convey the message that social science has accumulated con-siderable evidence on individuals' religious expressions. Certainly that voluminous literature has only been selec-tively sampled here, but a number of texts in the sociology of religion refer to dozens of additional sources. Our present task has not been to survey or review a range of data but to exemplify the special thesis of this chapter. As it stands now, most of what we know about how individuals express their religion has little to do with any theory of religion in society.

V

DILEMMAS OF CONTEMPORARY
RELIGIOUS ORGANIZATION

 To many people, the term "religious organization" may seem needlessly complex in referring
to what is simply the local congregation. But
the local congregation is no simple structure in
its own right, and an adequate treatment of religious organization would include much more. In fact, we face a major
problem at the outset in deciding just what aspects of the
topic should be covered here. The array is bewildering.
Surely there are differences between local lay organizations
concerned with church finances, church suppers, and recreation leagues, and, on the other hand, clergymen's associations and national professional staffs. Is there a major
distinction between the organization of the storefront sect

and that of the formal denomination? And what about the differences between denominations themselves? Many generalizations from the Congregationalists are riskily applied to Presbyterians and Lutherans, although Protestantism as a whole has characteristics in contrast to Catholicism and Judaism. In fact, Western religion is itself distinct when compared with many forms of non-Western and primitive religions. Indeed, the very importance of the topic "religious organization" is a mark of the West. To others around the world, the issue would evoke puzzlement, for their religion is seen and conducted on a wholly different plane. Where then should our present concern with religious organization start and stop?

From one perspective, the answer is obvious. This volume is directed to students—and, as everyone knows, the student is expected to know everything, as opposed to the scholar, whose area of expertise must be small to be legitimate. We do, after all, have a formulation of religious organization that has pretensions of offering everything. This is the fabled church-sect distinction, introduced in Chapter II. The first section here considers it again, calling upon more contemporary developments. But we shall argue that the distinction has only limited utility and shall seek an alternative perspective to govern the remainder of the chapter. This perspective has its roots in sociological theory rather than in theology. It has no singular reference to religious groups but is meant to apply to various organizations, whether they are religious, political, or economic. In this sense, the perspective is somewhat broader than the church-sect distinction, but in another sense, it is more limited. At least as we shall develop it, it refers primarily to the Protestant "church" on the assumption that a relatively detailed exploration of one form of religious organization is preferable to a loosely gathered net tossed over all forms.

The Legacy of the Church-Sect Distinction

Earlier we saw that the church-sect distinction embraces a number of concepts that are part of the Weberian legacy in the sociology of religion and that the distinction illuminates a good deal of the historical development of both Catholicism and Protestantism. The idealtypical "church" and "sect" differ in both internal and external characteristics. Externally, the church seeks to make its peace with the secular society surrounding it, whereas the sect is either aloof or hostile. Internally, the church has many of the earmarks of a bureaucracy with professionalized leadership, high valuation of ritual, and an impersonal evangelizing strategy that welcomes persons wherever and whatever they may be. The sect, on the other hand, is more of an amateurish social movement with lay, charismatic leadership, an emphasis on perfervid spontaneity, and a sense of religious exclusiveness as reflected in high membership standards. The sect offers high religious status to compensate those with low social status; the church recruits those with relatively high social status and seeks compatibility with the secular society that confers the status.

There is no doubt that the church-sect distinction has been crucial to the development of the sociology of religion itself. Nor is there any doubt that it still has much to recommend it. For one thing, so much work has been invested in the distinction that it provides a kind of scholarly continuity. For another, insofar as the distinction has been used to refer to the processes by which churches spawn sects that in turn become churches over time, its dynamic formulation has been to the sociology of religion what Marxian theory has been to the social sciences as a whole. Both offer models of change that are provocative in their breadth of application, their sense of historical inexorability, and their ability to bring together—if not unify—a host of specific variables and analytical considerations.

Certainly the church-sect dynamic has been applied to more than the early growth of Catholicism and the Protestant Reformation of the sixteenth and seventeenth centuries. As we noted in Chapter III, H. Richard Niebuhr has used the perspective in analyzing subsequent developments in Protestantism under the rubric of "the social sources of denominationalism," but more recent authors have used contemporary instances to elaborate and refine the framework. One major issue has been to distinguish among different types of sects according to their likelihood of evolving into churches. For example, some theorists have distinguished between sect and cult in that the former does tend to become a church over time but the latter does not. Others refer to an institutionalized sect as opposed to a church, suggesting that some sects merely institutionalize their sectlike characteristic rather than become full-blown churches. Still others distinguish church from ecclesia, in that the latter is more of a state religion with a more inclusive purpose and a more elaborate organizational structure.[1]

One contribution to this literature deserves special mention. Bryan Wilson has argued that the theological mission

---

[1] The post-Troeltschian literature offering theoretical modifications of the church-sect scheme is voluminous. The following are only a few of the entries: H. Richard Niebuhr, *The Social Sources of Denominationalism* (New York: Holt, Rinehart and Winston, 1929), pp. 16–21; Howard Becker, *Systematic Sociology* (New York: Wiley, 1932), pp. 114–118; J. Milton Yinger, *Religion in the Struggle for Power* (Durham, N.C.: Duke University Press, 1946), pp. 18–23, and J. Milton Yinger (ed.), *Religion, Society and the Individual* (New York: Macmillan, 1957), pp. 144–145; Peter I. Berger, "The Sociological Study of Sectarianism," *Social Research*, Vol. 21

of a sect helps to determine its likelihood of becoming a church and thus falling prey to organizational encrustations.[2] Wilson distinguished four essential types of sects: (1) the adventist (predicting and preparing for a sudden and drastic change in the world along apocalyptic and millenarian lines—for example, the Jehovah's Witnesses); (2) the introversionist (rejecting prevailing societal goals and positing new ones in their stead that call upon a different set of inner resources from the individual—for example, the Quakers and some Holiness groups); (3) the conversionist (optimistically seeking to change the world by altering individuals within it—for example, the Salvation Army and the Pentecostalist groups); and (4) the gnostic (accepting the prevailing societal goals but seeking new means for achieving them, based on esoteric doctrinal interpretations—for example, Christian Science and New Thought).

At the risk of oversimplification, we can summarize Wilson's argument this way: those groups that urge severe alterations in society itself are the least likely to become churches or denominations, largely because their antipathy to society precludes the churchly tack of appeasement. Thus, the radical adventist and introversionist groups tend to move only as far as the institutionalized sect. On the other hand, the more compromising conversionists and gnostics are more likely to become full-fledged churches,

---

(Winter 1954); Bryan Wilson, "An Analysis of Sect Development," *American Sociological Review,* 24 (February 1959), 3–15; D. A. Martin, "The Denomination," *British Journal of Sociology,* Vol. 13 (March 1962); Benton Johnson, "A Critical Appraisal of the Church-Sect Typology," *American Sociological Review,* 22 (February 1957), 88–92, and "On Church and Sect," *American Sociological Review,* 28 (August 1963), 539–549; and see the exchange between Erich Goode, N. J. Demerath III, and Allan W. Eister in the *Journal for the Scientific Study of Religion* (Spring 1967).

2 Wilson, *op. cit.*

though some are more likely than others. The conversionist sects are especially good candidates (as the histories of most current Protestant denominations attest) because their goals of conversion are oriented toward individuals rather than society at large and because of special factors concerning the typical conditions of their emergence and their internal structures. The gnostic sects are somewhat less likely to become churches because, although they do not seek to alter goals, their means are typically tied up in a highly developed and sophisticated doctrine that brooks no compromise. Moreover, gnostic groups are often the exception to the low-status rule among sects. Both the Christian Scientists and the New Thinkers are disproportionately middle class, and although this position might seem to lead them in the churchly direction of the middle classes generally, it may also give them sufficient strength to hold out against the pressures of the middle-class society around them.

Wilson's article is an extremely perceptive and wide-ranging analysis of the interplay between a group's values and its organizational attributes. But note that Wilson and others have departed considerably from the initial statements of church and sect as ideal types. More sophisticated questions have led to more sophisticated answers that carry far beyond the original insights of men like Weber, Troeltsch, and Niebuhr. This point can also be illustrated by two recent studies concerning who joins a sect and why sects retain their membership despite disappointments and abuse. The answer in the classic literature is that those of low status join to escape their secular burdens and reap the benefits of religious rewards. But this explanation is far too general, for only a minority of low-status people join. John Lofland's recent study of an adventist, millenarian "doomsday cult"[3] makes it clear that recruitment depends upon more subtle psychological stresses and penchants than status alone; it also depends upon the timing of the recruiting invitation in the individual's life history. Another study was more centrally concerned with why the members of such apocalyptic groups maintain their membership even after repeated failures of the apocalypse to materialize on the predicted date. Leon Festinger, Henry Riecken, and Stanley Schachter showed that when prophecy fails, membership commitment may actually be redoubled as a way of coping with the cognitive dissonance that is produced.[4] This observation touches on our discussion of cognitive dissonance and the institutionalization of religious sentiment in the previous chapter, but it also puts a point on the matter. That is, once people are committed to an unorthodox group with an unorthodox ideology, they often respond to rebuff by increasing their commitment instead of facing the loss of self-esteem entailed in backing off altogether. Thus, organizations frequently count on burning their members' bridges behind them.

Once again we find that the analysis of crucial aspects of religious organization depends on theories and insights that are foreign to the classic legacy of the church-sect distinction. But this is not only true of analyses of sects themselves. Indeed, general criticism of the church-sect framework has crescendoed in the last few years precisely because more and more students of "church" organization have found the traditional well dry. Some critics focus on

---

3 John Lofland, *Doomsday Cult: A Study of Conversion, Proselytization, and Maintenance of Faith* (Englewood Cliffs, N.J.: Prentice-Hall, 1966).

4 Leon Festinger, Henry W. Riecken, Jr., and Stanley Schachter, *When Prophecy Fails* (New York: Harper Torchbooks, 1965).

the logical liabilities of theory, because, like most ideal types, the church-sect distinction offers a hodgepodge of traits with little systematic notion of how—or even if—these traits are related.[5] It might also be suggested that the theory amounts to a self-fulfilling prophecy because we are cowed by its credentials and allow it to filter our observations so as to confirm its hypotheses. There is a further accusation that the theory tries to say so much that it winds up saying little at all. For example, it indiscriminately combines sociological and theological criteria and thereby illuminates neither.[6] Finally, a more recent group of critics would argue—perhaps with Weber himself[7]—that the framework is too singularly religious in character, thus cutting off analyses of religious groups from insights to be had from analyses of other forms of organization.[8] It is certainly true that sociologists of religion have tended to study churches on their own terms. There are few instances in which religious organizations are systematically compared with other forms of organizations, and it may well be that we can learn more about churches by examining the literature on business bureaucracies, political parties, mental hospitals, and the military than by burrowing deeper into the theologically based church-sect formulation.

This is obviously not the place for such a wide-scale com-

---

[5] See Goode, Demerath, and Eister, *op. cit.*, for discussion of these logical problems.

[6] See Berger, *op. cit.*, and Johnson, "A Critical Appraisal," *op. cit.*

[7] It is worth noting again at this point that although Weber is commonly referred to as the father of the church-sect distinction, he had a tendency to shunt the progeny to the sidelines when the real analytic work began, as in his later monumental work *The Sociology of Religion,* trans. Ephraim Fischoff (Boston: Beacon Press, 1963).

[8] For an elaboration of this point, see Demerath, *op. cit.*, and Charles H. Page, "Bureaucracy and the Liberal Church," *The Review of Religion,* 16 (1952), 137–150.

parative examination. At the same time, it may be appropriate to mark a beginning by suggesting an overarching perspective possibly suited to the task. Recognizing that we have learned a great deal from the church-sect legacy, let us also recognize that new frameworks are often the source of new insights. Indeed, the task of spinning out a new perspective may be provocative in itself.

Talcott Parsons: A-G-I-L in Behalf of Analytic Agility

To some extent the foregoing preamble has been misleading. We have promised a new perspective, but it is really only new in its specific application to religious organizations. The perspective is Talcott Parsons', and Parsons is certainly a sociologist to be reckoned with in contemporary theory. Over the past thirty years he has developed a general theoretical framework that is awesome in its scope[9] and variously interpreted. Surely the debate over Parsons is likely to rage on, and this is not the place for

---

9 Parsons has been not only provocative but prolific as well. A complete listing of his relevant works is clearly out of place here, but some of the more important include Talcott Parsons, *The Structure of Social Action* (New York: McGraw-Hill, 1937; reprinted New York: Free Press, 1949); *The Social System* (New York: Free Press, 1951); with Edward Shils, *et al., Toward a General Theory of Action* (Cambridge, Mass.: Harvard University Press, 1951); with Bales and Shils, *Working Papers in the Theory of Action* (New York: Free Press, 1953); with Bales, *et al., Family, Socialization, and Interaction Process* (New York: Free Press, 1955); with Neil J. Smelser, *Economy and Society* (London: Routledge, 1956); "Pattern Variables Revisited: A Response to Professor Dubin's Stimulus," *American Sociological Review*, 25 (August 1960), 467–483; and with Shils, Kasper Naegele, and Jesse Pitts (eds.), *Theories of Society*, 2 vols. (New York: Free Press, 1961). For a very lucid and useful summary of Parsons' intellectual development and trust, see Edward C. Devereaux, Jr., "Parsons' Sociological Theory," in Max Black (ed.), *The Social Theories of Talcott Parsons* (Englewood Cliffs, N.J.: Prentice-Hall, 1961), pp. 1–63.

another volley for or against.[10] Instead, we want simply to extract Parsons' most basic framework and develop it in our own fashion. Put another way, we shall use Parsons as a source of strategic questions without relying upon him for the answers. We plan to use his model as a way of organizing a search without relying on his hunches as to what will be found.

The basic Parsonian model is largely a response to the age-old question "What would be necessary for a society (or an organization) to achieve a 'stable equilibrium' in its affairs so that it does not succumb to what Thomas Hobbes once termed 'the warre of all against all,' and so that it is able to maintain itself over time?" At one level—and the only level we shall consider—Parsons' general answer is straightforward. Drawing upon the theoretical legacy of men like Weber and Durkheim and the experimental small-group research of Robert Bales,[11] Parsons posits four basic "system problems" that must be solved.

---

[10] The critical literature concerning Parsons and the functionalism he represents is central to post–World War II developments in contemporary sociological theory. See, for example, Black, *op. cit.;* William C. Mitchell, *Sociological Analysis and Politics: The Theories of Talcott Parsons* (Englewood Cliffs, N.J.: Prentice-Hall, 1967); N. J. Demerath III and Richard A. Peterson, *System, Change, and Conflict: Contemporary Sociological Theory and the Debate Over Functionalism* (New York: Free Press, 1967). Note, however, that Parsons himself has rarely dealt with the wider issues of functionalism per se; he has preferred to go about his own work in his own way. Moreover, criticisms of Parsons are frequently inconsistent with each other, partly because they criticize different works, and Parsons has changed considerably over time. Thus, a good deal of the criticism concerns *The Social System,* but this work is a poor representative at best of Parsons' current thinking and theoretical style.

[11] As abstract and macroscopic as Parsons' theory may seem, it is important to note that it was partly grounded in the beginning in Bales' empirical, small-group research. See Robert F. Bales' *Interaction Process Analysis* (Cambridge, Mass.: Addison-Wesley Press, 1950).

First, there is what Parsons terms the *latency* problem, or that of "pattern maintenance and tension management." Thus, every group must be able to motivate and mobilize its members even when they are faced with dilemmas and uncertainties. To do this, a society or organization will depend in the final analysis on its values and world view. It must socialize its members to accept them; it must continually reinforce the socialized commitment over time.[12]

But the problem with values and world views is that they are often too nebulous to serve as concrete goals for the day-to-day operation of a society or organization. Therefore, a second problem that must be solved is the translation of such values into goals and then the making of appropriate moment-to-moment decisions necessary for *goal attainment*. This is essentially a political problem, though formal political agencies are not the only agencies contributing solutions.[13]

So far, then, we have discussed two "system problems" that involve maintaining the basic identity of a society or

---

12 Insofar as religion is concerned with basic values and commitments, Parsons locates it in this L box of his fourfold scheme when the scheme is applied to whole societies. Note, however, that the alignment is not invariant. One can imagine societies in which religion is more appropriately analyzed in the I, G, or A box instead. Indeed, one of the major contentions of this chapter is that traditional religion is no longer consonant with the basic values of contemporary American society. Put another way, it is an aspect of society whose niche in the Parsonian scheme is undergoing change.

13 It should be noted that one of the prime difficulties of working with the Parsonian framework is a rather thoroughgoing sociological relativism. Parsons talks about abstract functions that must be fulfilled for stability's sake, but he is careful to avoid a strict parceling of particular structures and institutions to these functions. Thus, as footnote 12 indicates, religion may come under the L, I, G, or A heading, depending upon the society and the religion at issue. Because of this indeterminancy, it is difficult to make statements about actual structures that are not either indeterminate themselves or tautological, because structures are often defined in terms of the functions they are later "discovered" to serve.

organization and putting that identity into concrete action. The remaining two problems have to do with exigencies that may obstruct such aims. Parsons refers to these as the adaptive and the integrative problems. The *adaptive* problem involves maximizing one's relationship to the external environment, whether it is the physical environment, other societies, or other organizations. Because social units never function in a vacuum and because the environment may be especially threatening, the problem is crucial indeed.

Yet it is no less crucial than a further problem that rises from inside the society or organization itself, the problem of *integration*. Certainly one can imagine a group whose values are clear, whose goals are concrete, and whose external relationships are positive but that founders on the shoals of internal competition and conflict stemming from an ill-advised division of labor and a pervasive sense of social injustice. The integrative problem thus assumes major proportions on a par with the other three.

The four system problems outlined form the basis for Parsons' well-known fourfold scheme of boxes represented as A-G-I-L (see Figure 2). Suffice it to say that the scheme is only a beginning for Parsons' more refined theoretical analysis concerning inputs and outputs (or "exchanges")

A		G
Adaptation	Goal attainment	
Latency (pattern maintenance and tension management)	Integration	
L		I

Figure 2. Parsons' fourfold scheme of boxes represented as **A-G-I-L**.

between the boxes and between the subsystems within each box (since each box has its own lower-order a-g-i-l components; for example, there are latency, integrative, goal-attainment, and adaptive problems to be solved in those activities that are themselves Adaptive for the larger system). We shall not only eschew such details but shall also apply the general scheme to only a single institution within the society rather than to the society itself, as Parsons is wont to do. Note, however, that Parsons explicitly provides for applications at levels other than the society as a whole; indeed, it is fundamental to the comparative flexibility of his paradigm.[14]

Before we relate these abstract categories to the specific dilemmas of the religious organization, one further preliminary is in order. It is important to realize that Parsons does not offer these problem areas with the illusion that the problems are always solved; nor do we have such illusions for the church. Churches are no more utopian than any other organization when seen sociologically, and our approach is, if anything, the reverse of utopianism. Throughout the remainder of the chapter, we shall deliberately focus on tensions, dilemmas, pathologies, and points of strain within religious organizations. To some, this may appear distorted and even blasphemous. Yet it follows from a conviction that organizations cannot be realistically understood merely in times of harmony and in terms of their public face. Instead, they are best revealed at moments of crisis and conflict. It is precisely when irreconcilable alternatives clash that organizations are laid bare in their

---

14 For other examples of applying Parsons' theory to the analysis of organization, see Frances G. Scott, "Action Theory and Research in Social Organization," *American Journal of Sociology*, 64 (November 1958), 386–395; and Suzanne Keller, *Beyond the Ruling Class* (New York: Random House, 1963), especially Chapter 4.

fundamental priorities and preferences. It is especially under such circumstances that the actual structure of an
organization becomes apparent, in contrast to the formal
structures that are publicly proclaimed. Finally, insofar as
sociology can be construed as "helpful" to religion, its help-
fulness is much more likely to occur when the discipline is
used to probe rather than to celebrate. And so let us begin
the probing with the first of Parsons' four system problems.

Latent Religious Values in a Secular Society

One of the underlying assumptions of the church-sect
legacy is that although the sect's ideology is either
reclusive or rebellious, the church's values are compatible
with society and allow for not only rapprochement but perhaps even entanglement. This relationship is an important
reflection of the theological and historical roots of the
church-sect distinction itself. In fact, it is precisely these
roots and assumptions that make the distinction much less
applicable today. Thus, the distinction between church and
sect had been near the heart of Catholic theology long before it was first employed in scholarly usage, toward the
end of the nineteenth century. The notions of church and
sect were conceived at a time when the societal context was
itself more religious in tone and character than it is today,
at least in the United States. There is a very real sense in
which the traditional values and world views of *both*
church and sect are deviant in contemporary society. It may
no longer be possible for any traditional religious organization to swim in the societal mainstream.

There is, of course, an abiding paradox in considering
religious groups to be societal deviants. After all, the church
has long been a bastion of conformity and a moral tool in
the interests of social control and the reduction of deviance.

But let us be clear about what we mean by the concept of deviance itself. Certainly we do not mean to suggest miscreance, maliciousness, or rampant immorality, though, of course, these may also be found in the religious sanctuary. Rather, our primary argument is simply that traditional religious values are no longer consistent or wholly in tune with the pervasively secular emphasis in the contemporary culture. For example, the traditional Christian emphasis on revelation is at odds with the secular emphasis on rationality; a stress on ultimate, otherworldly salvation may be out of keeping with a Protestant Ethic gone berserk in which this-worldly attainments become valued for their own sake; Protestantism's own emphasis on "radical individualism" may grate against a secular society that puts increasing emphasis on the ethics of communal welfare and government regulations; and finally the very notion that religion should be a primary commitment of the individual runs counter to the credo of a pluralistic society that holds that an individual must have a portfolio of well-balanced allegiances so as not to become overcommitted to any one.

The important point here is not that these value positions are logically inconsistent, but rather that they are felt to be inconsistent by increasing numbers of people and parishioners. This is certainly the empirical message of the important and recent work of Charles Y. Glock and Rodney Stark, cited in the preceding chapter, on the individual and his religion. They suggest, for example, that a "maverick" such as Bishop James Pike among Episcopalians is really only a maverick with respect to the past, not the present. Pike himself has cited the study to indicate that a goodly proportion of lay Episcopalians seem to agree with his doubts and criticism concerning traditional doctrine. (In this light, it is worth noting that among the clergy, sociologists of religion are often damned as irrelevant; here two sociologists were at least relevant to the "damned.") Or consider the unusually dramatic Gallup poll data concerning religious influence in life, also cited in Chapter IV. Some 14 percent of a representative sample of Americans felt that religion was losing influence as of 1957; the proportion had mounted to 31 percent by 1962 and to 57 percent by 1967. Although such data can be variously interpreted, they certainly imply that religion has less and less in keeping with secular society. Insofar as traditional religious values and doctrine are deviant, the ramifications are important.[15]

Such a situation clearly threatens the basic religious identity and security of the church. Some response is called for, and at least four alternatives are currently observable, none of which is likely to be a panacea. Of course, one possibility is simply to ignore the matter or even to cultivate it in order to capitalize upon it. This approach has been the predictable, if uncalculated, response of most fundamentalist and sectlike groups. After all, these groups tend to recruit members who are alienated from the secular society in the first place; the greater the gap between the society and the religious group, the more the latter is able to benefit as an escape and a source of distinctive comfort.

But this strategy does not appeal to most religious organizations. Three other alternatives are more likely. The more radical of them is suggested by the controversy over the

---

[15] An increasingly important instance of the disharmony between the churches' values and those of secular society is seen in the ministry to higher education. In many respects, higher education represents values of the future, those toward which society generally will be moving. Churches, recognizing the situation, have in this century elaborated a special cadre of clergy to attend to the citizens of universities. But to the degree these clergy understand the secular aims and try to develop a ministry around them, the church fails to recognize and reward their efforts. See Phillip E. Hammond, *The Campus Clergyman* (New York: Basic Books, 1966), especially Chapter Five.

putative "death of God." Thus, many theologians and churchmen have begun to consider radical alterations in religious dogma so as to minimize its friction with the secular context. Of course, the process of change may be more important than any change itself, for it lends a new dynamism to religious affairs, belying the image of the church as a static institution nurturing the past and avoiding the future. But radical changes are difficult to agree upon,[16] and they have little widespread appeal. They produce short-run discomforts with no long-run guarantees. Surely there are less upsetting modes of modification available.

One of these lies in a third alternative response. Here the object is to secularize the doctrine so that it is both more appealing and less conspicuous. Of course, the response has taken both more and less sophisticated forms. On the one hand, there is the highly sophisticated theology of Paul Tillich and those who seek rapprochements between religious doctrine and intellectual orientations as diverse as psychoanalysis, Marxism, and existentialism. On the other hand, there is the more palpable bowdlerization of doctrine, as in Jane Russell's reference to God as a "living doll," the characterization of the former United States Senate Chaplin Peter Marshall, as "God's kind of guy," and the Protestant

---

16 From the perspective of the uninitiated, both radical politicians and radical churchmen are often seen as more homogeneous groups than they are in reality. Not only are there bitter differences between Stalinists, Maoists, Trotskyites, and so forth in the political realm, but there are also major differences between men like Pike and Hamilton in the theological galaxy. To make it clear that Pike is not a "death of God" theologian for all his putative "radicalism," see his exchange with William Hamilton in the letters column of *Playboy*, January 1967—an exchange that followed Hamilton's own rather good delineation of the "death of God" theology in the issue of December 1966.

radio spot that argues with conviction that "the blessings you lose may be your own."

But a fourth alternative is by far the most commonly invoked. Here the procedure is to leave traditional doctrine understated and, wherever possible, unmentioned. Like a bad joke, it is regarded as a sure death knell to good conversation. Like the proverbial skeleton in the closet, it can be an embarrassment to one's guests. Note that this strategy has several important consequences. First, it allows one to appear more conventionally religious than one actually is, and thus it may be especially appealing to many young and intellectually inclined ministers who would seem hopelessly irreligious to many of their parishioners were they to "tell all." Second, the response is a crucial ingredient in the omelet of ecumenism, because it leads to a minimization of religious differences and promotes what Martin Marty terms the fourth great American religious faith, "religion-in-general."[17] Of course, Marty is not alone in detecting this faith. Will Herberg saw and lamented it earlier as the identification of religion with American democracy so that the important thing was to have a religion, any religion, even without regard to creed, however mindful of race and color.[18]

These, then, are four alternative responses to the problem of harboring deviant religious values in a secular context. To some extent, the church is caught in an inextricable bind; it is "damned" if it does seek to reduce its deviance and "damned" if it does not. The former course risks a loss of basic identity and perhaps a small but important minority of adherents. The latter may risk the fate of an irretriev-

---

[17] Martin E. Marty, *The New Shape of American Religion* (New York: Harper & Row, 1958).

[18] Will Herberg, *Protestant, Catholic, Jew* (Garden City: N.Y.: Anchor Books, 1960).

able loss of relevance and a much larger group of actual and potential congregants. If Parsons is correct in noting a fundamental relationship between an organization's basic values, on the one hand, and the commitment and mobilization of its members, on the other, clearly the kind of alternative invoked is crucial. It is not only telling for the pattern that is to be maintained, but it is fundamental for both producing and resolving the tensions to be managed. This point should not suggest that most religious organizations consciously choose among the alternatives or even recognize the problem at issue. That one strategy occurs rather than another is partly a function of decision making, partly a function of the absence of decisions, and partly the unintended consequence of responses to the three other major dilemmas that we shall discuss below.

Unattainable Goals, Goallessness, and Goal Displacement

If man is goal directed, his organizations are doubly so. Crystallized goals not only distinguish organizations from idle collectivities and unruly mobs but also may provide the organization with a sense of destiny that transcends the fate of any individual within them. For Parsons, the problem of goal attainment has two principal components. First, concrete goals must be derived from and reinforced by the ultimate values of the system. Second, these goals must be pursued through a political structure of decision makers and executors. The contemporary church can be seen as disadvantaged in both respects.

We have just seen that the traditional values informing religious organizations in this country are somewhat deviant and precarious. It follows that goals derived from these values should be unstable as well, if only because they lack the legitimacy of being anchored in values wholly acceptable in themselves. Thus, the goal of securing ultimate, otherworldly salvation for individual members is strangely tainted. There are increasing numbers who simply do not believe—or do not believe saliently—in the premise behind the goal. The point is not that salvation is spurned, but rather that it may be losing its urgency.

There is a further problem with many of the traditional goals of religious organizations. We have already alluded to the importance of "concrete" and "crystallized" goals. This is because goals should provide clear directives for action and relatively unambiguous criteria for evaluating organizational success and individual contributions to it. But the traditional goals of religious organizations lack just this degree of specificity and therefore often fail to perform such functions. Even if salvation is seen as an urgent goal, how does one measure the extent to which it has occurred and how does one ensure that the proper steps have been taken? If God alone knows, then all but the most faithful members of the flock will have periods of doubt. Perhaps worse, the goal will become unrewarding precisely because the rewards are uncertain and postponed to another life, whose existence may itself be doubtful. Thus, striving for salvation may become an empty effort for many; it may actually reduce the organizational commitment of a large proportion of members.

Once again, however, it is possible to imagine several alternative responses—responses this time to a dilemma brought about by traditional goals that are low in saliency, uncertain, unmeasurable, and perhaps even unattainable. Here, as before, the most popular alternative is simply lack of action, in which case churches run the risk of goallessness itself. That is, one can easily imagine a situation in which the traditional goals lose their thrust but go unreplaced by any substitutes. The church loses its sense of purpose, begins to wallow in a kind of organizational anomie, and starts a process of atrophy that may culminate in organizational death itself.

This specter of goallessness is particularly haunting to organizational functionaries. Many are led to ward off the danger through one of two alternative strategies. The first is to seek goals that lie beyond the traditional impetus of the church but are concrete and crystallized in compensation. For example, many young ministers have begun to borrow goals from the civil rights movement, the skirmish against poverty, the antiwar movement, or, on the other hand, the John Birch Society and the causes of the right wing. Of course, many would argue that this borrowing is not as foreign to religious doctrine as we allege. After all, the church has always had a mandate to work within the world in order to change it. Although such involvement is certainly valid according to one reading of Western religion, the prevailing interpretation seems to be different. Certainly it is not easy for a minister to politicize his pulpit; there is a tendency for his parishioners to seek comfort within the church rather than using the church as an instrument for societal betterment.[19] In part, this use is a function of the

---

[19] The problems of politicizing a parish are well known to clergymen and sociologists of religion alike. For some of the literature in this area, see Ernest Q. Campbell and Thomas F. Pettigrew, *Christians and Radical Crisis* (Washington, D.C.: Public Affairs Press, 1959); Charles Y. Glock and Benjamin B. Ringer, "Church Policy and the Attitudes of Ministers and Parishioners on Social Issues," *American Sociological Review*, 21 (April 1956), 148–156; Charles Y. Glock, Benjamin B. Ringer, and Earl R. Babbie, *To Comfort and to Challenge* (Berkeley: University of California Press, 1967); Liston Pope, *Millhands and Preachers*, 2nd ed. (New Haven, Conn.: Yale University Press, 1965), especially the Introduction by Richard A. Peterson and N. J. Demerath III; Jeffrey K. Hadden and Raymond C. Rymph, "Social Structure and Civil Rights Involvement: A Case Study of Protestant Ministers," *Social Forces*, 45 (September 1966), 51–61.

process of structural differentiation, discussed with reference to the Protestant Reformation and the issues currently surrounding religion and the community. For whatever reason, it should be clear that this particular source of goals can be perilous. Not only does it run counter to the moods of most congregations, but it may also run the risk of straying irrevocably from the traditionally "religious" identity of the churches themselves.

A second alternative response may be safer in the short run but equally perilous over the longer course. The technical term for this alternative is "goal displacement," referring to the process by which the means to goals displace the original goals to become goals in themselves. To some extent, of course, such displacement is inevitable in any complex organization with a division of labor and a routinized, bureaucratically stipulated task allocation. But religious organizations may be especially vulnerable because their original goals are particularly vague and precarious. For example, we have already mentioned the sociological difficulties inherent in the theological goal of securing "salvation." The goal displacing adaptation might be one that makes a goal in itself out of recruiting members to the church. Originally recruitment was a means to the end of salvation, because the church was a source of the requisite grace and ethics. Over time, recruitment has detached itself from such theological aims, and the churches have begun to recruit for recruitment's sake alone. Some cynics have suggested that many contemporary churches are now involved in a numbers' game that goes beyond the bingo so common at church bazaars. The larger game concerns the competition for membership size, and the competition is anything but prizeless. Denominational budgets as well as community prestige are partly decided on the issue of size. After all, here is one goal for which success and failure can be empirically determined.

Yet empirical determinations may be at odds with other criteria for evaluating the church. Indeed, if recruitment occurs without regard to religious predisposition or inclination, it may pose a severe threat to the organization. Thus, the increased competition for membership between congregations and denominations has been a spur to more vigilant, and perhaps even to more distorted, bookkeeping when annual membership reports are handed over to the National Council of Churches for tallying. We argued in Chapter IV that many of the statistics seeming to support a post–World War II religious revival should be minimized for precisely these reasons.[20] Others have suggested that if competitive recruitment is what revival means, perhaps a decline would be preferable. For example, Peter Berger has suggested that the churches would do well to abandon their policy of indiscriminate evangelizing in favor of a "remnant theory" of religious organization in which the only members are the truly committed members.[21]

---

[20] For a discussion of the relationship between the increased competition for members and the alleged religious revival, see Chapter IV of this book and also Benson Y. Landis, "Confessions of a Church Statistician," *National Council Outlook*, Vol. 7 (February 1957).

[21] Three authors who confront the alternatives of the "remnant" concept versus "multitudinism" are Winthrop Hudson, Peter Berger, and Martin Marty. See Hudson's *The Great Tradition of the American Churches* (New York: Harper & Row, 1953), especially Chapter XI; Berger's *The Noise of Solemn Assemblies* (Garden City, N.Y.: Doubleday, 1961); and Marty's *The New Shape of American Religion* (New York: Harper & Row, 1959), especially pp. 117–121 and 134–157. Once again, however, there are differences among these boat rockers; they seem to rock in somewhat different directions. Hudson advocates the remnant notion; Marty maintains a qualified faith in multitudinism; and Berger is prepared to allow the parish to be almost anything if

Further consequences of goal displacement are especially important for an analysis of religious organization and the internal structures involved in making and executing policy. Note first that the process by which means become ends in themselves is generally a quiet one, without fanfare. The quietness itself is crucial, for it allows these new goals to develop momentum without careful monitoring, and the momentum may lead to unforeseen and unpleasant consequences that become institutionalized before they are detected. One of these consequences may be a differentiation and fragmentation of the church so that some of the most important functions are being handled by relatively autonomous functionaries who lack supervision and whose decisions and decision making are antithetical to the basic spirit of the religious group at issue. At the level of the local congregation, for instance, a banker may be recruited to serve as head of the finance committee because of his banking talents rather than his religious concerns; he is given a good deal of autonomy in exercising his expertise, and his decisions may shape church policy contrary to the wishes of the more religiously committed but less organizationally effective members of the laity. Or consider an example from the denominational level. Paul M. Harrison's classic study of the American Baptist Convention[22] reveals that missionary activity was one of a number of means-

---

other agencies of the church can begin to cultivate new directions and goals.

22 Paul M. Harrison, *Authority and Power in the Free Church Tradition: A Social Case Study of the American Baptist Convention* (Princeton, N.J.: Princeton University Press, 1959). Harrison, in fact, emerges with a new variant of Weber's three types of authority. In addition to the charismatic, traditional, and rational legal, Harrison posits the "rational pragmatic" to cover cases in which bureaucratization comes about not through formally announced codifications but rather through gradual and covert response to organizational exigencies.

become-ends that not only produced new divisions of authority in the denominational headquarters but forced a general change to an overall bureaucratic structure in a denomination with a fabled allegiance to the policy of "local congregational autonomy." This change occurred covertly over a number of years. Indeed, it occurred so slowly and so covertly that the deed was done before the general Baptist laity was aware that there were any changes at all in the wind.

Later we shall return to the problem of church polity in discussing the integrative dilemmas of the church. Meanwhile, two qualifications are important in concluding the present section. One of these is to correct any misapprehension that churches or religious organizations pursue only one goal at a time. It is true that we have tended to focus on single goals for the sake of simplicity, but in reality no church is that simple. If there are tensions surrounding any single goal, these tensions are surely multiplied in reality, where there are a number of different goals to be decided and acted upon. The problem of multiple goals is perhaps nowhere more clearly revealed than in the substantial literature on the role conflict of the minister, which we shall summarize briefly at the conclusion of this chapter.

Another qualification of this section, however, concerns another mistaken impression we may have cultivated. There may be a tendency to assume that only older religious organizations face problems with respect to goals because the problem is partly one of changing goals over time. And yet Donald L. Metz's recent study of six new suburban congregations[23] reveals that the dilemma is no less acute for them. Metz distinguished between "formal goals" (derived largely from formal doctrine) and "survival goals"

---

[23] Donald L. Metz, *New Congregations: Security and Mission in Conflict* (Philadelphia: Westminster Press, 1967).

(entailed in keeping the congregation going merely as an organization). He found that in all but one of the six congregations the survival goals quickly emerged as dominant. They were not only more immediately meaningful to the suburban parishioners but also more calculated to ensure maximal relations with denominational headquarters. Apparently, new churches as well as old must confront the dilemma. But then the dilemma is characteristic of organizations in general and not religious groups alone.

Adaptation and Adumbration

For Parsons, the adaptive problem involves coping with the external environment. Of course, much of the foregoing concerns adapting traditional religious values and goals to a secular society. But Parsons' notion of adaptation is somewhat more specific. The challenge is not merely to adjust to the context but also to manipulate it. The successful adaptation is one that reaps the benefits of the environment instead of merely avoiding overt conflict. Thus, Parsons' example of adaptation at the level of the society is the functioning of the economy in converting raw natural resources into usable goods. The analogue for the adaptive problem of the church has to do with recruitment, that is, converting individuals into church members. Certainly the problem of recruitment offers a clear-cut vantage point on the difficulties of the religious organization vis-à-vis its context. Precisely because recruitment has become so important as a result of goal displacement, special tensions are associated with it.

It is obvious but fundamental that individuals have only limited capacities for memberships and commitments that must be allocated among a host of competing organizations. Insofar as the church enters the competition, it has two quite different sorts of rivals: first, secular groups and agencies that perform a number of similar functions; and second, other churches and religious groups representing other denominations or other faiths. In both cases, the competition may be severe, forcing alterations within the competing church itself. But the two cases should be considered separately.

From a sociological perspective, the church is held to perform a number of functions for its individual adherents. These functions can be crudely divided into two basic groups: those concerned with answering the need for "meaning," and those concerned with "integrating" individuals with each other. As we saw in the preceding chapter, however, the church is hardly the exclusive fount of either function. As examples, the Rotary Club, an extended family network, a political party, and even one's occupation carry values that provide meaning in life and serve to place the individual in some sort of integrated relationship with others. It is true that the nature of the meaning and the framework for integration may vary, but this variation does not reduce the competition; it may even increase it. The church, we said, is frequently seen as a deviant institution, so it has special obstacles to overcome when forced to contest individual allegiances with secular agencies.

One plausible basis of accommodation between the churches and their competitors might involve scheduling commitments through the week. Thus, Sunday is reserved for the church, Monday for a business recreation group, Tuesday for the Rotary, Thursday for the PTA, Friday for a circle of group therapy, and Saturday for parental supervision of the Little League or television sports, depending upon whether one has a commitment to active or passive athletics. Yet an organization's thirst for the involvement of its members is not that easily quenched. Many of the church's most vital activities, ranging from sewing circles to the meetings of the board of deacons, are sprinkled through the week. Sunday is not enough, and yet, if the church makes demands on the rest of the week, it had better be on the rest of the week's own secular terms.

Examples abound to indicate that the churches are well aware of the problem and have adapted accordingly. Some offer psychiatric clinics;[24] many host nursery schools. Charles Page has referred to the "basketballization" of American religion[25] to suggest the proliferation of church recreation leagues to compete with secular recreational outlets. Or consider the case of the Crossroads Supper Club in Detroit, a former night club that now features gospel singing rather than torch songs and diet soda rather than alcohol. The response of one local clergyman was particularly noteworthy in envisaging a nationwide string of "Prayboy Clubs."[26] As further steps in this direction, there are already religious "drive-ins" for families unwilling or unable to leave their cars, church services on commuter trains to cater to the businessman on the go, and telephone access to "Dial-a-Saint," through which one enterprising businessman has made a good deal of money by providing

---

24 In this connection, it is worth considering the Protestant church in New York City that began a clinic in its basement, pooling the resources of pastoral counselors and outside psychiatrists. It happened that the only psychiatrists available were Jewish and that they ultimately drove out Protestant pastoral counselors on grounds of analytic incompatibility. Thus, it soon developed that a Protestant church was sponsoring a Jewish clinic and contributing to a double ecumenicism: first, between religious groups, and second, between religion and psychiatry.

25 Page, "Bureaucracy and the Liberal Church," *op. cit.*

26 Marc Raizman, " 'Night Club' Succeeds Without Liquor, Sexy Waitresses, Jokes," *Milwaukee Journal,* February 28, 1963.

a Biblical quotation followed quickly by a spot commercial for a local funeral parlor.

Such illustrations connote the process of secularization. But although many of these examples seem to make secularization tantamount to vulgarization, this is not necessarily the case. If there is any truth to the axiom that a meaningful religion must be relevant to its own time, certainly a modicum of secularization is necessary, and, in some societies, vulgarization may be the order of the day. Nor should the process of secularization be seen as clear indication of hypocrisy or prostitution. In this connection, it is worth recalling again the argument concerning an alleged religious revival in the United States. Proponents of the revival have their detractors among those who argue that secularization has occurred instead, but, of course, the same trend may reflect both processes at once. Thus, secularization of the sort we have described may be a *precondition* for any revival that has occurred, for it is only when the church changes sufficiently to compete effectively with alternative secular organizations that its membership is likely to increase. In this same vein, one of the seeming ironies of this allegedly secular age is that the churches have at least retained their numerical strength while such irreligious groups as the Unitarians, the Ethical Culture Society, and the American Rationalist Federation have, if anything, fallen behind in the competition. Note, however, that the relation between increasing church participation and irreligion may be closer than one might suppose. Thus, irreligious groups have been largely eclipsed by the willingness of the religious groups to relax their own standards of orthodoxy and adapt to more secular currents.

Here, however, we should pause to consider the relation between the *recruitment* of new members and the *com-*

mitment of old members. The two are not always congenial to each other.[27] First, in order to maintain the old members' commitment, it may sometimes be necessary to go to bizarre lengths to satisfy their needs. But this may frustrate the organization from successfully recruiting newer members whose needs and inclinations are more conventional. On the other hand, one of the risks of secularization as a means to an expanding membership is that some of the older, more traditionally inclined members will feel let down and even betrayed in the process. This is a recurrent theme among sects that compromise their doctrines in becoming churches. It may also be a source of tension within churches that compromise even further in a secular context.

Earlier we mentioned that the competition with secular groups was only one aspect of external adaptation. Another is the competition of any single church with those of other denominations and other faiths. The evidence suggests that this sort of competition is increasing. Mounting geographical mobility produces more free-floating adherents, and insofar as some churches find their membership size increasing, this growth is much more a matter of effecting denominational transfers than of evangelizing the formerly unchurched. The rise of "religion-in-general" indicates de-

---

[27] For further discussion of the difficulties inherent in maximizing both recruitment of new members and commitment of old members in a deviant organization, see N. J. Demerath III and Victor Thiessen, "On Spitting Against the Wind: Organizational Precariousness and American Irreligion," *American Journal of Sociology*, 71 (May 1966), 674–687. This article offers an organizational analysis of irreligion in general and the demise of one Wisconsin ethnic irreligious group in particular. But note that many of the processes and dilemmas that occur within irreligious groups can also be seen in religious groups as well. The two do not require radically different models, perhaps because both are deviant in a society that esteems "religion-in-general" but no longer appreciates traditional religious doctrine.

clining denominational loyalties, while the related, positive thrust of the ecumenical spirit also serves to minimize particularistic religious ties. It should therefore come as no surprise that the high-status Protestant denominations seem to be outcompeting churches of lower status. Part of this success is due to church affiliation's long-standing function as a status symbol, so that joining a higher-status denomination indicates either that one has "arrived" or that one is striving to do so. But such motivations are easily overestimated. Another compatible explanation is consistent with our prior discussion of secularization. High-status churches are apt to be less traditional in doctrinal content and doctrinal emphasis; they may also be more affluent[28] and hence more expansive in the range of secular services they can offer. Ironically, then, competition among churches is often resolved not in favor of the most religious but precisely in favor of the least.[29]

The competition itself, however, is not wholly unbridled; several forms of ecumenism serve to draw it in. First, denominational mergers are themselves mechanisms for reducing competition and its attendant costs, although it is true that some mergers occur between denominations

---

[28] But note that the affluence of a church is not necessarily related to the affluence of its individual members. Thus, some churches with low-status members are able to exact a relatively high proportion of their incomes through tithing and so forth. Other churches with high-status members find it difficult to get more than a very low proportion of their incomes. For an empirical examination of this topic, see Kenneth J. Lutterman, "Giving to Churches: A Sociological Study of the Contributions to Eight Catholic and Lutheran Churches," unpublished Ph.D. dissertation, University of Wisconsin, 1962.

[29] Note, however, that this discussion of membership competition is restricted to churches and does not include sects. Many of the latter, of course, have higher rates of growth than any church. Indeed, if the self-reported statistics are credible—a large "if"—sects generally have grown at a much faster rate than churches generally throughout twentieth-century America.

whose strengths are in quite different geographical regions (for example, the Eastern Congregationalists with the Midwestern Evangelical and Reformed). Second, a number of communities now host interdenominational churches that combine members from various denominations and sometimes combine wholly distinct denominations under the same roof, as often takes place in small towns suffering from a shortage of clergymen. Third, even where there are no mergers or interdenominational groups, the churches themselves often work out ground rules to minimize friction. Arthur J. Vidich and Joseph Bensman provide an excellent discussion of such arrangements in their *Small Town in Mass Society*.[30] Rules govern not only the religious allocation of newcomers to the community but also the ministerial participation in community ceremonies so that no one faith has an edge in public appearances. "Tacit antipoaching agreements" are well known and reinforced among the local clergymen, although several families posed "jurisdictional disputes" that required bargaining and virtual litigation.

In all this, it is important to underscore the point that ecumenism can be seen as a collective response to problems felt by denominations separately. Increasing discussion of ecumenism may be seen as making a theological virtue out of an organizational necessity. This point holds not only for the adaptive problems but also for the previous issues concerning values and goals. Thus ecumenism is not merely an exemplification of the axiom "safety in numbers" but also serves to emancipate denominations from their historical

---

[30] Arthur J. Vidich and Joseph Bensman, *Small Town in Mass Society* (Garden City, N.Y.: Anchor Books, 1960), especially pp. 245–262. For a more general discussion of contemporary forms of ecumenicism, see Robert Lee, *The Social Sources of Church Unity* (Nashville, Tenn.: Abingdon Press, 1960).

legacies, thus facilitating some of the adjustments that we have reviewed.[31] Moreover, ecumenism provides further aid in the form of increasing bureaucratization, leading to a greater proportion of administrative staff and a wider social distance between the staff and the laity at the parish level. From the standpoint of some laymen, this last development may be anathema, particularly in denominations that have long esteemed the principle of local parish autonomy (several abortive lawsuits were filed against the Congregationalist Church authorities by laymen anxious to prevent the merger with the Evangelical and Reformed Church), but most laymen are either indifferent to or supportive of these steps. Certainly, most denominational officials regard the growth of bureaucracy and increasing social distance as benefits. The officials are allowed to posit and pursue new programs with a minimum of traditional interference. They are more protected from sticky confrontations with nonprofessional church members. They are able to recruit innovative staff members who are more anxious to serve the denomination's "Southeast Asia desk" or its "campus ministry" than a suburban pulpit. Although ecumenical mergers are often more illusory than real at the level of the local parish, the reality is keenly felt at the top and, not surprisingly, by the very people who negotiated the merger in the first place. From one perspective, ecumenism is a way in which the suborganization of denominational officialdom can adapt to a crucial aspect of their external environment —the parishes themselves. But this issue is clearly related to integration.

---

31 This may be one answer to the question raised by a recent empirical analysis of belief differences among clergymen of different denominations and their implications for ecumenism. See Jeffrey K. Hadden, "A Protestant Paradox—Divided They Merge," *Transaction*, 4 (July–August 1967), 63–69.

The Integrative Problem Through the Eyes of a Clergyman

℘ If a researcher were confined to analyzing only one of Parsons' four problems and sought the one that would best predict and reveal underlying tensions and difficulties in the church as a whole, his choice might well be the integrative "box." Here is where many of the previous issues come home to roost. No one is more aware of this than the minister in charge. In fact, his daily routine involves him in crucial and agonizing integrative problems of two sorts. First, there is the integration of the church's various activities and hence the minister's various roles. Second, there is the need to integrate the church's various parishioners, the minister's variegated clients, and the denomination's various types and levels of structure.

One of the best replicated findings in the literature on religious organization concerns the role conflict of the clergyman. Because the clergyman is formally the ranking functionary of his parish organization, his conflict may be conflict that afflicts the organization as a whole. Samuel Blizzard has pointed to five basic roles that tax the minister in different ways and push him in different directions.[32]

---

[32] Samuel Blizzard, "The Protestant Parish Minister's Integrating Roles," *Religious Education,* 53 (July–August 1958), 374–380. The further literature in this area is summarized well in Oliver R. Whitley, *Religious Behavior* (Englewood Cliffs, N.J.: Prentice-Hall, 1964), especially Chapter 7. See also James M. Gustafson, "The Clergy in the United States," *Daedalus,* 92 (Fall 1963), 724–744; Joseph H. Fichter, S.J., *Religion as an Occupation: A Study of the Sociology of Professions* (Notre Dame: University of Notre Dame Press, 1961); Jerome Carlin and Saul Mendlovitz, "The American Rabbi: A Religious Specialist Responds to Loss of Authority," in Marshall Sklare (ed.), *The Jews* (New York: Free Press, 1958), pp. 377–414; and Marshall Sklare, *Conservative Judaism* (New York: Free Press, 1955), especially Chapter VI. All this literature is important, but many of its insights can be had

First, there are the obligations of *preacher* and *priest,* involving sermonizing from the pulpit and administering sacraments and ritual, respectively. Then there is the role of the *community-relations man,* in which the minister must front for the church and participate in community affairs and ceremonies. Fourth, there is the expectation that he will serve as *pastoral counselor,* providing private help to individual parishioners undergoing crises. Finally, there is the *administrator* syndrome, in which the clergyman must attend to the exigencies necessary to provide for the survival and growth of the church as a "mere" organization.

This ordering of the roles is not random. For one thing, they are roughly ordered by the amount of attention they are accorded in the clergyman's seminary training. This is especially true of the older seminaries, which concentrate on the traditional tasks of the minister, leaving him to grapple on his own with the psychological problems of pastoral counseling and the business and personnel issues of administration. Although the new seminaries, tied increasingly to major universities, give more preparation in these latter two roles, apparently the preparation is still not enough. The competence of the clergyman to handle these roles remains low when contrasted to his ability as preacher, priest, and even community-relations specialist.

But—and here is the most abrasive rub—the roles are also ordered according to the increasing amount of time that the minister spends on each. Blizzard's research reveals that the average church-based clergyman spends 40 percent

---

quickly and delightfully from another work of a different character, a book that should be at least recommended reading in every course on the sociology of religion. As proof that good satire and good sociology sometimes make splendid bedfellows and bedtime reading, see Charles Merrill Smith, *How to Become a Bishop Without Being Religious* (Garden City, N.Y.: Doubleday, 1965; reprinted by Pocket Books, 1966).

of his time on administration, 25 percent on pastoral counseling, 15 percent on community relations, and 20 percent on the combined functions of preacher and priest. Thus, often the minister spends most of his time on the roles he is least equipped for and finds most distasteful. He spends the least amount of time on the roles he is most prepared for and longs to cultivate further.

The task of integrating these roles and activities becomes further complicated when the parishioners themselves are consulted. Charles Y. Glock and Philip Roos reported that the church laity agree with the minister in their preferences for his role allocation.[33] They dislike the minister's spending a disproportionate amount of time on nontraditional roles having to do with administration; they prefer to have their clergyman devote most of his time to the preaching and priestly functions. Although some parishioners would no doubt welcome greater pastoral counseling, others now regard this as something in the professional domain of the psychiatrist, the lawyer, or the physician. Many would like to see community relations further developed, but others regard the minister's participation in the community suspiciously as a departure from the ideal conception of the church as an enclave unto itself. The clergyman, then, is caught in an uneviable bind. He is forced to spend most of his time on roles for which he is poorly equipped and about which neither he nor his parishioners are excited. Thus, he gets little reinforcement, and even if his expertise were great, it would be tainted and somewhat illegitimate.

But what of the problem of integrating people rather than roles? One common stereotype of religious organizations—whether of sects or of churches—is that their pa-

---

[33] Charles Y. Glock and Philip Roos, "Parishioners' Views of How Ministers Spend Their Time," *Review of Religious Research*, 2 (Spring 1961), 170–175.

rishioners are homogeneous brethren with common purposes, needs, and commitments. Like most stereotypes, this one is vulnerable to reality. Even sects are confronted with heterogeneity in the dispositions and inclinations of their members. Heterogeneity increases greatly among churches,[34] partly because of the sort of pell-mell recruiting that frequently occurs. There are important differences in the religious needs and penchants of high-status versus low-status parishioners, men versus women, old versus young, those with families versus those conspicuously without, those raised in a faith versus converts from another religious tradition, and those who view the church as a secondary affiliation reinforcing other primary commitments in secular society versus those who see the church itself as primary with all else paling beside it. None of these differences should be a surprise, but the problem is that all these types tend to coexist uneasily within any single denomination, any single congregation, and perhaps even any single committee or activity within that congregation. For one example, we often think of Episcopalians as exclusively high status. Although it is true that they have a peculiarly high proportion of high-status parishioners compared with other denominations, it is also true that more than 40 percent of the nation's Episcopalians are from the working and lower classes.

---

[34] For further discussion of membership heterogeneity and the minister's "role set," see Whitley, *op. cit.*, pp. 154–165 and Demerath, *Social Class in American Protestantism, op. cit.*, p. 182. The latter work argues, however, that heterogeneity may be a blessing in the long run, though a short-run curse. This is particularly the case with *status* heterogeneity among members, which affords the church a variegated membership with which to enact a division of labor and a balancing of directions in church planning. Indeed, Demerath argued that the greater stability of the churches, as opposed to the sects, may be due less to the higher social status of church members and more to the increased status variety in the church's membership.

Seen from the perspective of the minister, such variety produces a problem of "role set" alongside his difficulties with "role conflict." The former refers to the various audiences the minister must confront in discharging any one of his roles. For example, to which of the above should he pitch his sermons? Should he orient to one group one week and another the next? To which should he cater in decisions concerning ritual, for some find it overbearing and unnecessary but others wish to devote a substantial portion of the budget to an elegantly appointed altar and a choir that is actually on key? The same dilemma applies to the community-relations role, especially where the issues are political. Should he be "liberal" or "conservative" with respect to a local bond issue, a problem of busing students to parochial schools, or a liberalization of the local statutes concerning abortion? Surely pastoral counseling is affected, because the minister must be able to judge what sort of counseling will be most effective for what sorts of clients. Finally, even administration is buffeted. The minister relies upon presumably democratic committees, but frequently he must make appointments to these committees and resolve their stalemates. He must also represent committee decisions to the parish at large, even when these decisions are made by an unrepresentative group picked for its secular expertise rather than any particular measure of religious devotion.

In sum, the integrative problem can be severe in a local parish, especially insofar as that parish is involved in processes of intended and unintended change, and especially from the perspective of a clergyman caught in the vortex. But, of course, local parishes are members of larger denominational bodies, and this relationship presents another facet of the integrative problem to which we have already alluded. There are three classic models of the relations between the local parish and the denomination at large. One is the Baptist and Congregational model of *local parish autonomy*, in which the parish has the right to make all decisions relevant to it, including those concerning the hiring and firing of its ministers. A second model characterizes the Presbyterians, with rather small *regional denominational bodies* controlling most power plays. The third model is the Catholic, Episcopalian, and traditional Lutheran conception of a national denomination with a concentration of power in large *clerically run headquarters*. We have already seen two examples of processes by which these models break down in reality. Thus, the Baptists have moved to a national bureaucracy despite their ideology of local autonomy; and various mergers have increased the role of national officials among the Congregationalists. An opposite example of convergence might involve the splintering of the Lutheran church both ethnically and regionally as indicated by the persistence of Swedish versus German Lutheranism and the "Wisconsin" and "Missouri" synods. Yet the triple distinction is sufficiently maintained to require quite different forms of analyses for the particular denominations involved.

Consider, for example, the plight of the Southern white minister who wants to speak out as a liberal on race relations.[35] If he is a Baptist, his job is in the hands of his parishioners, and speaking out may lead to a kicking out. If he is a Presbyterian,[36] he is only slightly better off, because his employment is decided by a regional, partly lay, body—in this case, Southern—a body that may be only somewhat more moderate than the local parish. But if the minister is

---

[35] For references to this literature, see footnote 19 above.

[36] In some ways, the Methodist polity approximates the Presbyterian model, as explored in James R. Wood and Mayer N. Zald, "Aspects of Racial Integration in the Methodist Church: Sources of Resistance to Organizational Policy," *Social Forces,* 45 (December 1966), 255–265.

an Episcopalian, who is responsible to clerical headquarters in the North rather than to his parishioners, he is likely to get more support. Even here, however, the situation is hardly calculated to give comfort. On the one hand, his headquarters may like him to be a liberal; on the other hand, his local friends and parishioners may exert contrary pressure that is sometimes highly sophisticated. Speaking out may not involve the loss of his job, but it may mean preaching to empty pews.

Once again, then, we find the minister caught in the midst of poorly "integrated," conflicting forces. Just as he is bedeviled by factions within his own parish, he is also bewildered by the friction between the parish itself and his denominational headquarters. It should come as little shock, therefore, to find that the minister's role of community-relations specialist is seldom interpreted prophetically or politically. As the next chapter will indicate, the church and the minister are generally poor bets to stand at the vanguard of social change. Indeed, the ultimate irony that afflicts the minister can be seen with reference to the church-sect dynamic. At the sectlike stage in a denomination's development, the mood is ripe for bold and innovative prophecy, but there is no provision for a professional leadership. It is only when the churchly stage is reached that the professional clergyman is brought in, but this is precisely the stage at which prophetic wings are most severely clipped. Now he must contend with more heterogeneous adherents, a more bewildering organizational network, and the ever-present admonition to provide his members with more comfort than challenge.[37] Thus, he is invited into the

---

[37] This dilemma over "comforting" versus "challenging" is most easily seen in the role of minister, of course, but it also besets the church as it chooses any strategy. For an example of the dilemma cast in these terms, see Phillip E. Hammond, "Aging and the Ministry,"

religious arena only after the most spectacular action has been tamed and routinized. His primary objective is keeping the peace, but even peace is hard to come by in a setting in which brethren are sometimes only distantly related. Finally, the minister loses still more leverage in a secularized context that increasingly denies his traditional trump card of divine grace and inspiration. His religious status has declined even while his professional responsibilities have increased.

Summary

This chapter has sought to portray the nature of religious organization by viewing its problems. After examining the literature and legacy of the church-sect distinction, it sought an alternative orientation in the systems approach of Talcott Parsons. Using Parsons' four "system problems" as a framework, the chapter explored the difficulties associated with deviant religious values in a secular society, goallessness and goal displacement, adaptation and the competition for members, and the integrative dilemma from the vantage point of the clergyman himself.

In none of this discussion have we argued that the church is either peculiarly prone to problems or doomed to decay and ultimate death. Of course, the church has some problems that are especially pronounced, but many of its dilemmas are shared with other organizations of wholly different stripe. As for the problem of demise, every age has had its Cassandras warning of the decline and fall of the church.

---

in Matilda White Riley and John W. Riley, Jr. (eds.), *Aging and Society* (New York: Russell Sage Foundation, 1968), wherein ministering to old people through the local parish versus ministering to them through regional or national programs is posed as, in important respects, incompatible.

Even if such prophecies are more numerous and more strident today, they risk confusing change and readjustment with death itself.

It can be argued that there are two mechanisms for binding people in common concert: first, a distinctive ideology; and second, a centralizing structure of roles and authority. To some extent, these two are alternatives. Where one is present, the other is less crucial; where one loses force, the other becomes all the more important. Surely different religious groups can be categorized according to whether their emphasis is on ideology or structure, for example, the sect versus the church. But even among churches themselves, one might predict that as the distinctively religious doctrine or ideology begins to ebb, organizational structure will become correspondingly more urgent. In short, it may be that the decline of religion will be associated with the growth of the church as an organizational entity—one that is ever more committee-laden, professionalized, and bureaucratic. It is certainly true that the church is far different now from what it was a century ago and will be a century hence, but it is probably also true that "religion" as we have known it is likely to disappear long before the church as we are coming to know it. In this spirit, it is appropriate to conclude with a vignette that Karl Marx cited, perhaps with a special gleam in his skeptical eye: "When the Puritans at the Council of Constance complained of the dissolute lives of the popes and wailed about the necessity of moral reform, Cardinal Pierre d'Ailly thundered at them: 'Only the devil in person can still save the Catholic Church, and you ask for angels.' "[38]

---

[38] Karl Marx, *The Eighteenth Brumaire of Louis Bonaparte,* excerpted, for example, in Lewis S. Feuer (ed.), *Marx and Engels: Basic Writings on Politics and Philosophy* (Garden City, N.Y.: Anchor Books, 1959), p. 345.

VI

FORMS AND FRUSTRATIONS OF RELIGIOUS INFLUENCE IN CONTEMPORARY SOCIETY

Churches obviously have consequences for society. They provide services, occupy persons' time, spend money, take stands on issues, provide employment, use up space, and transmit knowledge. Sometimes they issue threats of damnation or promise health and well-being. Organizations doing such things are clearly in a position to *influence*, as well as *to be influenced by*, various community spheres.[1] The range of influences, indeed, is broad and includes not only results that religion intends but also results not intended and per-

---

[1] For example, the final five essays in J. W. Smith and A. L. Jamison (eds.), *Religious Perspectives in American Culture* (Princeton, N.J.: Princeton University Press, 1961), provide many illustrations of religious consequences for American novels, poetry, music, and architecture.

haps not even recognized. If celibacy, for example, is upheld as an ideal and encouraged among many as divinely ordained, then alterations in marriage practices and birth rates are not difficult to identify. But housing arrangements and inheritance patterns might also undergo modification, results not even seen let alone foreseen.

In Chapter IV, we discussed how religious involvement may have *individual* consequences. And in Chapter V, the internal, *organizational* facet of religion was analyzed. Now we turn to religious forces as they reverberate throughout the community and society, singling out two "functions" for special consideration. One of these, stemming from the Durkheimian tradition, is the cohesion or integration that society is presumed to enjoy as a result of religion; the other, arising from the Weberian tradition, is religion's prophetic role. The first sees religion as the way by which society's members unite, heal their interpersonal abrasions, and sanctify their solidarity. The second focuses on religion's part in social change, as a source of challenge and new interpretation. Thus, one view of religion conceives of it as largely a conserving force in the community; whereas the other sees it as largely liberating in its thrust. In this chapter, we examine both the "conservative" and the "liberal" aspects. Before we turn to either, however, it is appropriate to reintroduce a notion implied in Chapter I and discussed in some detail in Chapter III—that of structural differentiation.

Differentiation and the "Church" in Primitive, Premodern, and Industrial Societies

Differentiation shares with evolutionism the perspective that change occurs in society and that most change is from simple arrangements to more complex. But differentiation denies two other features of the evolutionary perspective—that the change is inexorable and that it represents "progress." Rather, differentiation simply acknowledges the increasing complications that arise from population growth, territorial gain, scientific sophistication, and the like. Societies can be seen as located somewhere along a continuum of structural differentiation, from very simple to very complex.

Let us imagine three hypothetical locations on such a continuum and thus three hypothetical types of society: one primitive, another premodern, the third industrial. Some societies are so "deviant" that they resemble none of the three, but most societies can be thought of as being approximations of primitive (small and homogeneous) or premodern (large and homogeneous) or industrial (large and heterogeneous). Following the discussion in Chapter IV of the institutionalization of religious sentiments, we can observe the form taken by the resulting "church" in each type of society.

Only in a figurative sense does a church exist in the primitive society. Religious sentiments pervade social life in small, homogeneous societies; their institutionalization is so bound up in other patterns of life that a separable "church" is not identifiable. The political leader, or the dominant figure in the kin group, may also be the overseer of religious activities. Economic transactions may be surrounded by sacred requirements, as may the planting of crops, the matching of mates, or the conduct of recreation or warfare. Sacred places and special occasions for being at those places may, of course, be designated, but activity at those times and places is not "voluntary"; persons are not readily classifiable as more or less religiously "active." Differential religious involvement reflects prescribed differences in age, status, political office, and so forth, not differences in "religiosity."

Given the religious situation in primitive society, therefore, it is difficult to assess the relationship between religion and the community. It is comparatively intimate, pervasive, and mutually supportive. Identifying this mutual support function was Durkheim's great insight, leading to the oft-stated dictum that the function of religion is to provide cohesion for the society: persons are morally bound to each other, and religion is their way of manifesting and reaffirming their commitment to the moral bonds. Take away religious expression, and the moral bonds would weaken; reduce the moral "density" or cohesion of the society, and the necessity of expressing religion would be less.[2] In one sense, then, in the primitive-type society the church *is* the community, or, more accurately, the community is the vehicle through which religious sentiments are expressed. Religion is both integrative and prophetic, both conservative and productive of change.

The premodern society differs from the primitive in that separate structures, identifiable as churches, exist in settings where populations are larger and economies, family arrangements, politics, educational agencies, and so forth are more delineated. Jut as many other activities are distinguishable, so are religious activities. Categories of priest and

---

[2] If the analysis in Chapter I is correct, the necessity of expressing religion would only lessen, not disappear, because there are other sources of religious sentiments than simply the moral bonds persons feel—death and natural cataclysms being two examples. The "church" and religious institutions in the primitive society are presumably capable of manifesting the full range of religious sentiments from whatever source. Later in this chapter we shall be raising the question of whether or not in modern societies the various "religious" sentiments are separately institutionalized, with the modern church manifesting largely philosophical sentiments, as pragmatic, ethical sentiments are located elsewhere. See Chapter I for the distinction between the two kinds of religious sentiments.

layman, active and nonactive, believer and nonbeliever are likely to arise; separate buildings and separate times for conducting sacred activity are likely to develop; formal rules specifying religious behavior tend to replace informal traditions.

Premodern societies, like primitive societies, are religiously homogeneous, however. Dissenters are removed through death or banishment, which indicates a signal characteristic of such societies: political and religious institutions are interwoven. Like Julian Sorel in Stendhal's *Le Rouge et le noir,* persons seeking power and prestige may elect political office or church office, and if the two are not equivalent, at least exchange of personnel between them is frequent. With cardinals or high priests serving as royal advisers, with local churches serving as tax and vital-statistics offices, with the political and religious regimes generally supporting each other, it is not difficult to see how "religion" relates to "community." The more involved are persons in the church, the more involved they are in community affairs. The more they favor religion, the more they favor the political arrangements in the society. The more they believe the orthodox doctrine, the more they believe in the legitimacy of the current regime. Because, in other words, there is but one religion in premodern society, and it is "established," it is probably correct to say that religion lends cohesion to the community and society. Without the church, the political regime would more often be challenged, but so also, without political support, the church would face competition and lose some of its effect on the community.

The last sentence provides a clue to the religious situation in modern societies. Being both large and religiously heterogeneous, modern societies are differentiated (so there is a separate, identifiable "church" structure) and pluralistic (so many different churches exist). The consequence is that the relationship between religion and community is neither pervasive (as in the primitive society) nor "established" (as in the premodern society).[3] Rather, their relationship is exceedingly clear at several points and exceedingly vague at others. Tracing through that relationship must be done by steps.

The Church and "Civil Religion" in the Cause of Societal Integration

The issue of religion's role in societal integration, perhaps more than any other issue in the sociology of religion, is complicated by a peculiarity we noted earlier —that "religion" and "church" tend to be equated in the American mind. But as we have insisted at several points, such an equation can be misleading. Just as not everything about churches is religious, neither is everything religious reflected only in churches. One way to see this point is to imagine modern society *without* churches.

Without churches in the United States, for example, would there be no worship, prayer, or devotional life? Would there be no admonition from respected persons or no inspirational oratory or no presentation of ideals? Would instruction of children disappear? Would welfare service no longer exist? Would persons in conflict have no place to turn for a decision of right or wrong? Would opportunities for people to manifest their commonality be absent? Would, in short, any of the things that churches might do not be

---

[3] Though he tentatively distinguishes five stages where we have used but three, Robert N. Bellah's essay "Religious Evolution," *American Sociological Review*, 29 (June 1964), 358–374, has again served as a source for our discussion here.

done if churches did not exist? Whether or not these things might be performed differently is not the question, for it seems quite obvious that all of the functions served by churches are functions that either are or could be served elsewhere as well. Churches instruct children, but so do public schools. Churches inspire, but some persons find inspiration in political ideology or fraternal lodges. Churches dispense clothing, soup, and job information; they give legal advice, counsel distraught persons, and sponsor basketball leagues—but so also do governmental and private agencies, from Social Security to Legal Aid to physicians and to the Police Athletic League.

The point of all this discussion is not to show how dispensable churches are but rather to point up how dangerous it can be to assume that the social structures through which various functions are served are the *only* social structures through which those functions *can* be served. The function at issue here is the integration of society. Although it has been argued that "religion" serves this function for primitive societies, we must not naïvely assume that the social structures we most readily call religious in modern societies function in the same way or to the same extent. The issue, as we saw in Chapter I is Durkheimian, but the present task is to examine the degree to which Durkheim's thesis is apt not for the Arunta of Australia but rather for our own complex setting. What is the relationship between "religion" and "social integration" in the modern society?[4]

A basic item of agreement among functional social theorists (if not all social theorists) is that for a society to

---

[4] It is clear from Durkheim's intellectual career that he would have extended his analysis of "elementary forms" to more complex societies, thus closing the circle begun with his *The Division of Labor,* had his final years not been involved with other work.

remain a viable social system its members must possess, or at least think they possess, a common set of values or aims. As Kingsley Davis stated it: "It is the possession of common-ultimate ends that gives the key to the integration of ends in human societies. . . . As between two different groups holding an entirely different set of common-ultimate ends, there is no recourse."[5] The point being recognized is that, short of brute force, people conduct their affairs because they trust each other, and trust implies a *common* acceptance of the higher aims toward which activity is directed. If one signs a legal contract, for example, there is the implication that the police power of the state can enforce the contract, but there is the further implication that police power is accepted ("trusted") as legitimate. How does real or imagined agreement on "common-ultimate ends" come about? Or, assuming the effectiveness of at least minimal socialization, how are the common-ultimate ends enhanced, manifested, and activated at critical times? A traditional answer, from Durkheim onward, has been that religion, in its beliefs, moral code, and ritual, serves this function; worship, regardless of what else it does for individuals, helps solidify the society by articulating and making "real" the ultimate aims of the worshipers.

But whether or not the *church* serves this function can clearly be questioned in the pluralistic society, where worshipers are engaged in worshiping differently. Members of group A may have their commonality enhanced by worshiping together, as may members of group B; but surely A and B are not thereby welded together. It is dubious, in other words, that American society, for example, is held together because there are Protestant churches, for there are also

---

[5] Kingsley Davis, *Human Society* (New York: Macmillan, 1950), p. 143.

Catholic churches, Jewish synagogues, and many persons who enter none of them.[6]

The key to understanding the resulting situation may be, however, not to see modern society as without social structural support for its moral unity (and thus without integration) but rather to see modern society as having alternative structural arrangements for performing this function. There may be, to borrow a phrase, a "civil religion."[7] In the United States, such civil religion has been called the religion of democracy, the common American faith, the American way of life, and, pejoratively, syncretism or American Shinto. Building upon the Judeo-Christian heritage (a cliché whose prominence reflects its impact on virtually all ideologies in the West), this civil religion has its own saints, sacred literature, symbols, places of worship, and social structures for handling moral questions. In America, the bulk of these religious institutions may be said to be located

---

6 Thus giving rise to charges that America is "post-Protestant," "post-Christian," or even "postreligious." See, for example, Roy Eckardt, *The Surge of Piety in America* (New York: Association Press, 1958); Martin E. Marty, *The New Shape of American Religion* (New York: Harper & Row, 1959); Gabriel Vahanian, *The Death of God* (New York: Braziller, 1961). Phillip E. Hammond, "Religion and the 'Informing' of Culture," *Journal for the Scientific Study of Religion*, 3 (Fall 1963), 97–106, is a critical review of this body of literature.

7 Robert N. Bellah, "Civil Religion in America," *Daedalus*, 96 (Winter 1967), 1–21; reprinted in Donald Cutler (ed), *The Religious Situation* (Boston: Beacon Press, 1968). The concept, as well as the phrase, is old. In the context of American society, a number of recent works have explored its meaning. See J. P. Williams, *What Americans Believe and How They Worship* (New York: Harper & Row, 1952), Chapter 14; W. Warner, *American Life: Dream and Reality* (Chicago: University of Chicago Press, 1953); Will Herberg, *Protestant, Catholic, Jew* (Garden City, N.Y.: Anchor Books, 1960). Still, Bellah's is the best identification of the phenomena under examination here, and some of the structural implications of his treatment and the issues discussed here will be found in Phillip E. Hammond, "Further Thoughts on Civil Religion in America," appearing, along with the Bellah essay, in Cutler, *op. cit.*

in the apparatus of government, and probably this transfer from religious to political institutions of civil religions is characteristic of modern societies.[8] In any event, the specific content of America's civil religion is most clearly seen on political ceremonial occasions. For example, consider the following excerpts from Andrew Kopkind's cynical report of the Presidential Prayer Breakfast, an annual Washington event:

> In government no less than in trenches, there are no atheists. Piety is the glue of politics, and no politician passes up the opportunity to proclaim his faith in a Higher Constituency. The Presidential Prayer Breakfast, and its sister meeting, the Congressional Wives Prayer Breakfast, represent the highest expression of official religious sentiment. The year's hard work—stamping "Pray for Peace" on envelopes and shouting "under God" loudly in the Pledge of Allegiance—finds its natural climax in the reaffirmation of national prayerfulness by the President and his First Lady, in witness before members of the Cabinet, the Supreme Court, Congress, the Diplomatic Corps, the active and retired Military, Industry, Science, Labor, Education.
>
> . . . This year's breakfast began sharply at eight, with the U.S. Army Chorus's rendition of "Sweet Hour of Prayer," and the invocation by Lieutenant General M. H. Silverthorn (USMC, Ret.), another permanent fixture at the meetings. Breakfast consisted of a lavish succession of delicacies, starting with a half-pineapple wrapped in blue cellophane. It did not, unfortunately, suit all. Representative Spark M. Matsunaga of Hawaii discerned immediately that the fruit had come not from his home but from

---

8 "It would seem that the problem of a civil religion is quite general in modern societies and that the way it is solved or not solved will have repercussions in many spheres." Bellah, "Civil Religion," *op. cit.*, p. 13. See also David E. Apter, "Political Religions in the New Nations," in Clifford Geertz (ed.), *Old Societies and New States* (New York: Free Press, 1963), pp. 57–104.

Puerto Rico, and he pushed it aside with distaste. His tablemates had to work quickly to restore the fellowship. Soon, however, the guests were immersed in breakfast lamb chops, creamed brains and fried potatoes, and before they knew it Senator Carlson was telling them about the success of the "prayer breakfast movement."

. . . The most moving speech of the morning was given by the Army Chief of Staff, General Harold K. Johnson, who told of his personal confrontation with God in several tight spots in the Pacific theater and during the Korean War. Finally, the President gave a short, curiously defensive address. The year before, in his maiden appearance as the President at the Presidential Prayer Breakfast (he had previously been there as Vice President), he had stirred many imaginations with a suggestion that the capital erect a "monument to God," alongside those to Washington, Lincoln, Jefferson and Robert A. Taft. Perhaps he felt the sting of cynical jibes, for this year Mr. Johnson sought to disarm the critics: "In our history it has been popular to regard with skepticism the private motives of public men and never more than when they participate in meetings such as this. I'm sure such skepticism has been deserved by some. But I am certain that only the unknowing and the unthinking would challenge today the motives that bring our public officials together . . . for prayer and meditation."

. . . Some who attended the breakfasts out of amusement, courtesy, or self-advancement, may be overcome with embarrassment as they watch ambassadors and their aides endure the morning pieties. It may be some comfort to know, then, that most of the foreigners find the display no worse than boring and not devoid of a certain native charm, such as Occidentals find in Oriental inscrutability. "You've got to admit, after all," says one foreign diplomat who has been to the breakfasts over the years, "that there is something terribly American about it."[9]

---

[9] Andrew Kopkind, "The Power of Prayer," *The New Republic*, March 1, 1965, pp. 19–20. Reprinted by permission of The New Republic, © 1965, Harrison-Blaine of New Jersey, Inc.

But lest we interpret Kopkind's humor as an indicator of insignificance, we can turn to Robert N. Bellah, who has relied on other sources and other occasions to offer a more serious historical delineation of America's civil religion:

> The words and acts of the founding fathers, especially the first few presidents, shaped the form and tone of the civil religion as it has been maintained ever since. Though much is selectively derived from Christianity, this religion is clearly not itself Christianity . . . The God of the civil religion is not only rather "unitarian," he is also on the austere side, much more related to order, law, and right than to salvation and love . . . He is actively interested and involved in history, with a special concern for America. . . . [T]he president's obligation extends not only to the people but to God. . . . The will of the people is not itself the criterion of right and wrong. There is a higher criterion in terms of which this will can be judged; it is possible that the people may be wrong. . . . [T]he rights of man are more basic than any political structure and provide a point of revolutionary leverage. . . . [The civil religion] provides a transcendent goal for the political process . . . [and] the obligation, both collective and individual, to carry out God's will on earth. . . . God's work must be our own.[10]

It might be thought that, because many of the founding fathers were "deists" and none of the first seven Presidents was formally a church member,[11] this emerging civil religion was a purposively designed *substitute* for Christianity. This position overstates the matter. More feasibly, the development of a civil religion in modern societies can be attributed to structural circumstances, especially differen-

---

[10] Bellah, "Civil Religion," *op. cit.,* pp. 7, 4, 5. We have liberally transposed these sentences.

[11] Leo Pfeffer, *Creeds in Competition* (New York: Harper & Row, 1958), p. 29.

tiation and pluralism, which force the separate institutionalization of the essentially pragmatic from the essentially
philosophical aspects of religion. The designers, in other
words, were responding to events of their day as well as
their own insight in intending civil religion to coexist with
other religions that were to be restricted to the doctrinal
realm only. As Salo Baron noted about one of the founders
of the American system: "Jefferson conceded . . . that in
their 'Metaphysical' aspects religious bodies might differ
widely, but demanded that as social organizations they
should all conform to the new political patterns of American
democracy."[12]

Such a demand as Jefferson's was presumably not to
spare the feelings of a tiny minority of non-Christians then
in America, but rather to safeguard the liberty of all citizens
to *believe* what they would. As Justice Holmes put it:

> *Persecution for the expression of opinion seems to me per-*
> *fectly logical. If you have no doubt of your premises or*
> *your power and want a certain result with all your heart,*
> *you naturally express your wishes in law and sweep away*
> *all opposition . . . But when men have realized that*
> *time has upset many fighting faiths, they may come to*
> *believe even more than they believe the very foundations*
> *of their own conduct that the ultimate good desired is*
> *better reached by free trade in ideas—that the best test of*
> *truth is the power of the thought to get itself accepted in*
> *the competition of the market. . . . That at any rate is*
> *the theory of our Constitution.*[13]

The critical phrase here is "come to believe even more
than . . . the very foundations of their own conduct." For
if a society is to be composed of persons free to hold what-

---

[12] Salo Baron, *Modern Nationalism and Religion* (New York: Harper
& Row, 1947), p. 41.
[13] Abrams vs. United States, 250 U.S. 616.

ever metaphysical postulates they will, and when at the same time conduct cannot be left ungoverned, then procedures for governing conduct must be accorded priority over the metaphysical postulates. That is to say, what in Chapter I were called the "ethical religious sentiments" tend to become structured apart from philosophical postulates or "cognitive religious sentiments." The latter still reside in religious organizations called churches, but the rules of general ethical conduct become institutionalized chiefly in the religiopolitical realm, emerging as the hagiocracy and shrines in Washington, D.C., patriotic oratory, political platforms, court decisions (especially from the Supreme Court[14]) arbitrating ethical conflict, legislatures establishing new codes of behavior, and so forth.[15] Of course, not all

---

[14] Max Lerner, "The Constitution and the Court as Symbols," *Yale Law Journal*, 46 (June 1937), 1290–1319. Paul A. Freund, *The Supreme Court of the United States* (Cleveland: Meridian Books, 1961), after discussing opposing "philosophies" of court behavior said, "The consensus that is required is only an agreement on secular, political principles. . . . That this political philosophy is consistent with a self-confident orthodoxy in matters of belief is the teaching of thoughtful religious spokesmen" (pp. 82–83). Our point, though not disagreeing with Freund's, is that calling for agreement on "secular, political principles" is itself "religious" spokesmanship. See also p. 114, where he compares Tillich's "Christian mediating principles" with the principles of judicial review. The extent to which the public at large "reveres" the court has been called into question by Kenneth M. Dolbeare and Phillip E. Hammond, "The Political Party Basis of Attitudes Toward the U.S. Supreme Court," *Public Opinion Quarterly* (Spring 1968).

[15] Though it would be incorrect to imagine that there is no disagreement at critical locations. In the U.S. Supreme Court and among jurisprudential writers, for example, one faction has contended with another over the proper role of courts in deciding conflicts, a contention that partially reflects the jurisprudential issue of "natural law." If there is a natural law, then courts must know it and apply it. If there is no natural law, then on what grounds do courts decide? A new interpretation of "natural" in this debate, an interpretation very much in keeping with the civil religion discussed above, is given by Lon L. Fuller, *The Morality of Law* (New Haven, Conn.: Yale University Press, 1964).

members of our society are committed to their civil religion (any more than all of Durkheim's Arunta were committed to their totems), but a significant majority doubtlessly are.[16] More important, persons strategically located in the "political" and leadership spheres are especially committed.[17]

If we now return to the basic Durkheimian issue of religion in the role of societal integration, it is probably correct to view America's civil religion as the proper analogue to the Arunta religion of which Durkheim wrote. Religion, broadly conceived, does indeed play a role in integrating society, but such religion is not to be confused with "churches" as they are commonly identified. Although churches not infrequently celebrate civil religion, their position here is not unique, for virtually all other organizations in the society participate in the celebration as well.

Still, three important qualifications to this thesis help to provide a linkage to the chapter's next section. For one, allegations that the churches are only concerned with a religion in general are unwarranted if the implication is that there are no theological differences between churches. Indeed, it is precisely such differences, and the climate permitting them, that create the pressures for a common civil

---

16 Will Herberg gives great weight to free, public education in producing Americans committed to American civil religion. "Religion and Education in America," in Smith and Jamison, *op. cit.*, pp. 11–51. Littell observed that some who do not accept the democratic, civic religion, that is, "spokesmen for the radical right, such as Robert Welch, Carl McIntire, and George Wallace, have attempted to make defense of 'Christian America' . . . a major bulwark of reactionary politics." Franklin H. Littell, "The Churches and the Body Politic," *Daedalus*, 96 (Winter 1967), 31.

17 As demonstrated, for example, by Samuel A. Stouffer, *Communism, Conformity, and Civil Liberties* (Garden City, N.Y.: Doubleday, 1955), and Herbert McClosky, "Consensus and Ideology in American Politics," *American Political Science Review*, 58 (June 1964), 361–382.

religion in the first place, that is, for a source of unity in the midst of diversity. Second, it is important to recall that the development of a civil religion has reflected events outside of the churches rather than decisions of the churches themselves. Although Jefferson and others preferred the churches to be restricted to a philosophical rather than a pragmatic role, not all of the churches have agreed, and many continue to be concerned about pragmatic political and ethical issues to the point of seeking specific and distinctive impact on the society at large.[18] Such positions, of course, relate to the church's prophetic role, which we shall consider next. But a third qualification is that even if the churches are little involved in integrating the total society, they remain concerned to unify their own members. In fact, this ambition to internal integration sometimes gets in the way of the prophetic role itself, as we shall see.

Prophecy Ventured and Unventured

It is convenient to divide religion's relationship with society into the integrative and prophetic functions, but like most conveniences, this one oversimplifies. Prophecy, for example, can be subdivided into *direct* and *indirect* influence or into *innovative* thrusts versus efforts to return to the *status quo ante*. For our purposes in this chapter, the most important distinction is between *efforts* and *success*, between prophecy *attempted* and influence *gained*. The first question, being largely a matter of the internal characteristics of the church as an organization, was touched upon in Chapter V, but we shall explore it further here. The latter

---

[18] This overstates the point, as we shall see. Rather than actually seeking to exert an impact, most churches and churchmen develop a sense of guilt for not having done so.

question requires a different analysis, which we reserve for the next section.

Every church, every theology, has some conception of the good life and, therefore, some conception of how people should behave. For some, "goodness" arises from eschewing as many secular obligations as possible; for others, active involvement in community affairs is virtuous. For some, the rewards after death are randomly allocated or achieved through special negotiations with church officials; for others, only an ethical life on earth can yield heavenly rewards; and for still others, doubt exists about life after death, so the motive for leading an ethical life comes from elsewhere. Weber's scheme, discussed in Chapter II, for classifying doctrines into otherworldly or this-worldly and into ascetic or mystical is one way to point up the obvious differences among churches in terms of their theological directions. But it was one of Weber's great contributions to raise the correlative question: "Given the direction a theology may take, where does it lead?" To some observers, churches have little influence because they attempt so little. Speaking in 1842, Francis Wayland noted that in churches "men are told how they must feel, but they are not told how they must act, and the result, in many cases ensues, that a man's belief has but a transient and uncertain effect upon his practice."[19] What was true in 1842 is certainly as true in the present day.

Doctrine is obviously central to the issue, but doctrine plays more than a direct role in helping to determine the community-oriented aims of religious organizations. In addition, doctrine exhibits subtle, indirect features that create

---

[19] Quoted in Sidney Mead, "American Protestantism Since the Civil War," *Journal of Religion*, 36 (January 1956), 4.

dilemmas for the church's prophetic inclination. For example, a theology points to many kinds of righteousness; so, in the case of any given situation, the problem of specifying which "good" takes priority is difficult indeed and makes the church's community rule unclear. Second, the question of authority to dictate members' actions, though always a matter with which doctrine deals, is a question of considerable confusion in its application, because every directive limits the freedom of members to make their own decisions. Third, the dilemma of charity arises over the twin aims of professing to speak to all men and professing to show a better way: is it better to bear prophetic witness or minister to all persons regardless of their sins? Thus, theological doctrine may provide guidelines for moral or communitarian action, but it does so in frequently ambiguous ways.[20]

The strains arise, of course, not from doctrinal dilemmas alone but also because a church's membership reflects to some degree society's vested interests: membership is the earth contained in treasured vessels. Who, for example, is to decide whether or not influence will be exerted? Perhaps the clergyman; but, as we have seen, the clergy are in precarious positions in many congregations, especially those doing their own hiring and firing. Reflecting, then, the friction that is always possible between religion's integrative and prophetic functions, the church is afflicted with an almost inherent fragility. If one mark of prophecy is boldness, ecclesiastical consensus is vulnerably brittle to prophecy itself.

In general, therefore, one can expect churches to be conservative more often than they are innovative, to follow society more often than they try to lead it. As an illustra-

---

[20] See the discussion of these dilemmas in Daniel Callahan, "The Quest for Social Relevance," *Daedalus*, 96 (Winter 1967), 158–159.

tion, or perhaps an extreme case, of this proposition, consider the research of Ernest Q. Campbell and Thomas F. Pettigrew on religion in a racial crisis, a study of local white Protestant ministers during the Little Rock, Arkansas, school desegregation struggle in 1957.[21] This research documents a general pattern of inactivity on the part of Little Rock clergy. Even though the events were overwhelmingly prominent in the community (and in the nation), and the ministers therefore felt obliged to comment on them from the pulpit, Campbell and Pettigrew indicated that rhetorical strategies typically were used, providing pseudoprofundity in the midst of careful neutrality. These strategies ranged from a strict emphasis on "law and order" to a stress on "deeper issues" going beyond the specific matters at hand. Although some ministers came close to an antisegregationist position with the "segregationists-are-stupid" technique, most who did so required a mechanism such as the "exaggerated Southerner" strategy, which distinguished them from carpetbagging Yankees and won sympathy from Confederate parishioners.[22]

Yet the point is not to demean those clergy but to elucidate their situation. We are not suggesting that they were peculiarly lacking in either courage or judgment. Many felt quite strongly that it was better to provide tempering sermons to full houses than to wax radical before empty pews. Others regarded their pulpit behavior as less important than their quiet integrationist activity behind the scenes. We are primarily concerned here with the structural conditions permitting prophecy, however, and in this connection it is worth citing some fourteen propositions offered by Campbell and Pettigrew by way of summary:

---

21 Ernest Q. Campbell and Thomas F. Pettigrew, *Christians in Racial Crisis* (Washington, D.C.: Public Affairs Press, 1959).

22 *Ibid.*, pp. 100–104.

1. The support of desegregation is less in times of racial crisis than in times of noncrisis. . . .

2. The support of desegregation during a crisis is not . . . directly linked to social class. . . . [Although the higher the status of the denomination, the more likely the minister is to favor desegregation, high status does not necessarily produce liberal *activity* on the part of ministers during a crisis.]

3. The more popular the denomination in the local area, the less likely are its ministers to defend positions not accepted by local public opinion. . . .

4. The minister is less likely to support desegregation during a crisis if no ministerial figures of high prestige in his denomination lead the way. . . .

5. With an increase in the number of years that the minister has served his congregation, there is a decrease in the probability that he will support desegregation during a crisis. . . .

6. The minister is less likely to support desegregation during a crisis period if he is over 50 than if he is under 40. . . .

7. The minister's support of desegregation is less if his church is engaged in a membership drive, building program, or fund-raising campaign. . . .

8. Given two churches of comparable size and drawing members from the same class, the one a neighborhood church and the other a community-wide church, the pastor of the latter is the less likely . . . to support desegregation during a crisis period. . . .

9. The minister whose orientation is primarily to his parish is less likely to support desegregation than the minister who is oriented to the community at large. . . .

10. The more stable the membership of his church, the less likely is the minister to support desegregation during a crisis period. . . .

11. The freedom of the minister to defend desegregation is more restricted if he was born and educated outside the South. . . .

12. The less personally affected are the members of a congregation by the issue, the greater is the freedom of the minister to support desegregation during a crisis period. . . .

13. Success (speaking numerically and financially) in the ministry is negatively related to the probability of strong advocacy of unpopular imperatives during crisis periods. . . .

14. Ministers in the small, working-class sects will support segregation and many of them will be publicly active in its defense.[23]

Most of our analysis so far suggests, then, that religious groups are unlikely to be a source of agitation in the wider society. Does this state of affairs not seem strange in an era when so much is heard and written about the new breed of radical churchmen, whether the iconoclastic theologian or the politically alert activist in the religious organization? Certainly radical preachments have for a long time issued from *sects*. Indeed, appealing largely to the disadvantaged, sects have good reason to communicate a kind of urgency as a way of maintaining members' commitment, even if their proposals are often more apocalyptic than realistic. Although it is true that few radical pronouncements or

---

23 *Ibid.*, pp. 121–126.

activities come from the pulpits of mainstream churches,[24] there are nevertheless sources of churchly prophecy that are removed from the pulpit.

In Chapter V, we mentioned the kinds of relationship that can exist between parish clergy and their denominational headquarters. Where the minister-headquarters line is tenuous—that is, where his employment is contingent upon his autonomous parish—local circumstances are more likely to minimize his prophetic efforts than in the case where a minister's employment is more under the jurisdiction of regional or national church officers. Extrapolating that point, we can propose that denominations will be radical or prophetic more often through their nonparish personnel, at times of national conventions when parish personnel are away from direct surveillance by the local parish, or in the midst of ecumenical bodies lying beyond the control of any single denomination. Let us consider these three conditions in order.

Concerning the nonparish personnel, two recent studies are especially relevant. Phillip E. Hammond and Robert E. Mitchell have shown that the Protestant campus ministry offers a case study of the "segmentation of radicalism."[25] Campus clergymen are unquestionably more liberal or less traditional than their colleagues in parish settings. To some

---

[24] This situation gives rise to an irony neatly portrayed in J. Milton Yinger, *Religion in the Struggle for Power* (Durham, N.C.: Duke University Press, 1946). Because the church has more members than the sect, and especially more high-status members, its potential influence is *greater*. But its attempts to exercise that influence are *less*. Because the sect's membership is smaller and consists more of low-status persons, its potential influence is much less than its vigorous demands on society would suggest.

[25] Phillip E. Hammond and Robert E. Mitchell, "The Segmentation of Radicalism: The Case of the Protestant Campus Minister," *American Journal of Sociology*, 71 (September 1965), 133–143.

degree this difference arises from more radical ministers "selecting" themselves into campus work, but in other cases radical ministers are siphoned off the parish structure to avoid embarrassment and strained relations with parishioners. These ministers are put instead in campus settings with which their radicalism more easily blends. From such positions, they are freer to speak "prophetically," to join causes, and so on. Moreover, whatever radical impact campus ministers have on students who return as adults to parish membership represents an indirect radicalizing of the church's conventional structure, perhaps a kind that could not take place directly.

A similar finding emerges from Jeffrey K. Hadden and Raymond C. Rymph's investigation of the clergymen who participated in the Chicago demonstrations concerning de facto segregation in the public schools.[26] They found *campus* clergy to be at the vanguard, and they support the more general point that nonparish clergy of all sorts are more likely to be involved than those who are in conventional pulpits. The "death of God" movement provides a different illustration of the same point; here is a radical thrust that is largely initiated and sustained by faculty members in theological schools and by high-ranking church officials who have a bureaucratic wall of protection between them and their denominations' laity. Indeed, the rapid growth of church bureaucracy, charted empirically by Gibson Winter,[27] has had profound meaning for the church's prophetic and innovative efforts. Bureaucratization does not

---

26 Jeffrey K. Hadden and Raymond C. Rymph, "Social Structure and Civil Rights Involvement: A Case Study of Protestant Ministers," *Social Forces,* 45 (September 1966), 51–61.

27 Gibson Winter, "Religious Organizations," in W. Lloyd Warner (ed.), *The Emergent American Society* (New Haven, Conn.: Yale University Press, 1967), I.

always signal timidity and rigidity; in this case, it has had opposite effects.

Denominational conventions represent a second structural channel through which churches may make prophetic pronouncements. By taking convention positions on political or moral issues of the day—such as recognition of Red China, civil rights, and abolition of capital punishment—denominations "speak to" the society in ways they frequently cannot through parish pulpits. Indeed, there is a sense in which the stridency of convention statements is a self-conscious compensation for the lack of stridency in home churches; the cloak of anonymity facilitates speaking out in this case. For example, Campbell and Pettigrew noted that many silent clergymen in Little Rock were genuinely sympathetic to desegregation efforts, a sentiment that surfaced during national meetings. Or consider Liston Pope's analysis of preachers' responses to the mill strike in Gastonia, North Carolina, in 1929. Local ministers were bound, largely economically, to the mill owners and thus felt compelled to oppose the strikers. Yet, many of these local preachers participated in statewide denominational conferences that arrived at policy statements deploring the mill owners' actions.[28]

Some issues, of course, are more likely than others to prompt prophetic positions. Here the work of Charles Y. Glock and Benjamin B. Ringer on the Episcopalians is especially relevant.[29] The Episcopalians have a bicameral convention scheme, with a house of bishops and a house of

---

[28] Liston Pope, *Millhands and Preachers,* 2nd ed. (New Haven, Conn.: Yale University Press, 1965).

[29] Charles Y. Glock and Benjamin B. Ringer, "Church Policy and the Attitudes of Ministers and Parishioners on Social Issues," *American Sociological Review,* 21 (April 1956), 148–156.

lay representatives and lower-order clergy. Glock and Ringer were able to compare the final decision of the convention with the individual sentiments of the Episcopalians represented. One finding was that the church is most likely to take bold positions on matters on which the parishioners are themselves split or heterogeneous in their views. This pattern can be interpreted in two ways. Either it means that the church seeks out controversy and then confronts it aggressively, or it means that the church only speaks out on issues where there is little chance of mass opposition from a united laity. Undoubtedly, there is a little of both involved, but a second major finding of the study lends further credibility to the latter, more skeptical interpretation. Thus, the church is not likely to deviate from the views of its parishioners on issues where the laity have direct self-interests. It is one thing to be radical on the recognition of Red China or the need for crash activity in Southern civil rights; but it may be quite another to talk about racial open occupancy in Northern housing or to issue strong proclamations on economic matters that will adversely affect many businessmen.

A third, and relatively new, structural device facilitating prophetic stances by churches is the ecumenical movement. Ecumenical bodies are removed not only from the local scene but also from specific denominational histories. It is no accident that the clearest beginnings of church involvement in social protest in this country, the so-called social-gospel movement, coincided both with the first steps of ecumenism and with the emergence of "segmented" campus clergymen. Out of these moves came the Federal Council of Churches (now called "National") and the larger World Council of Churches. Although it is true that the social-gospel movement was not as radical as is sometimes alleged,[30] placing as it did considerable emphasis on "conversion" as an antidote to poverty, nevertheless it called attention to the poor and was sufficiently challenging to antagonize many church members. Thus, the Federal Council provided an ecumenical organizational base for the prophetic religious movement of its day, just as the present National Council of Churches supports such ventures as the Delta Ministry—a group of clergymen operating a radical civil rights mission in Mississippi. An ecumenical movement is in one sense an emancipating measure; and, as Weber pointed out, emancipation is a crucial condition for the emergence of religious prophecy.

How, then, to summarize these reflections on the condition of prophetic departures? Perhaps the following distinction will help concerning the responses to religious differentiation in society at two levels of religious organization itself. At the level of the local parish in the local community, the response is typically one of trying to restore the unity that differentiation has threatened. Thus, many congregations are working hard to keep the peace with various community institutions in order to legitimize themselves as organizations, to further their efforts at recruitment, and to maximize their chances of attaining internal integration for a heterogeneous membership. From this perspective, adventuresome prophecy constitutes dangerous boat rocking.

On the other hand, the situation of the nonparish religious personnel is quite different. To these people differ-

---

[30] Several excellent historical assessments of the social gospel movement include Henry F. May, *Protestant Churches and Industrial America* (New York: Harper & Row, 1949); Donald B. Meyer, *The Protestant Search for Political Realism, 1919–1941* (Berkeley: University of California Press, 1960); and Robert Moats Miller, *American Protestantism and Social Issues, 1919–1939* (Chapel Hill: University of North Carolina Press, 1958).

entiation offers an advantage rather than a liability. Instead of seeking to retreat from autonomy back to a more integrated state, they prefer to use the autonomy as a condition for saying and doing things that would be stifled by such integration. It is not that integration is undesirable but rather that its priority ranks below that of prophecy, especially among those who are not responsible for running a parish. In sum, at the local level parish there is an "escape from freedom" in the interest of religion's integrative function; at the national, nonparish level there is an inclination to take advantage of the freedom in the interest of religion's prophetic function. As we shall see, however, neither path is without its brambles when one asks what religion actually accomplishes as opposed to what it attempts to accomplish.

The Conditions of Prophetic Influence

Prophecy can, of course, be nothing but words. It is one thing to identify the conditions under which prophecy will emerge and another to identify the conditions under which it will have influence. In this final section, therefore, we raise the question "So what?" When is the church likely to effect changes in the community and the society?

A first group of variables here concerns the type of influence at issue. Despite the many connotations of terms like "radical" and "prophetic," we have been using them in a neutral sense to signify any message the church might issue that calls for alteration in society. But the crucial questions here are how much alteration, in what direction, and against what resistance? Is the demand for a wholly new social order, a return to some prior form of society, or something in between? Does the demand reinforce or contradict the sentiments of the church's parishioners? How does the mainstream of society itself feel about the issues? Is it moving in that direction anyway or is the demand wholly inconsistent with current societal trends? A quite different factor concerns whether the attempted influence takes an indirect path, seeking to modify the behavior of individuals—thence the entire society—or whether it takes on the society directly, working straightaway at the centers of power. And third, through what organizational forms is the influence channeled? Are national bureaucracies more effective than local parishes? Parish clergymen more than nonparish clergymen? We cannot, to be sure, supply definitive answers to queries of this sort, but they serve nevertheless as the framework for our basic question: Just what difference does the church make in society?

We noted earlier that church influence is more likely to be conservative than innovative because of the church's need to maintain stable relationships with and among its parishioners. It is worth noting, therefore, that much of what passes for prophecy is really reinforcement of existing sentiment, whether from a conservative or a liberal perspective. Even church statements that are prophetic from the standpoint of the wider society will often turn out to run with, rather than against, the sentiments of particular religious congregations. Thus, many of the most radical churchmen—whether for or against civil rights, poverty, or war—are acting not so much as prophets in the wilderness as followers of their own lay frontiersmen, offering legitimacy and sophistication. A cynical view of this situation is seen in a Congregational clergyman's remark during his community's imbroglio over a "planned parenthood" campaign. "The pastor's position on a religious issue," he said, "can have influence only to the extent that laymen regard the position as their own."[31]

The importance of such "prophetic reinforcement" should not be underestimated, however. First, efforts to assign priority to prophetic statements can be a fruitless task; often their coherent articulation by an established institution is as important as the fact of their first utterance. Second, by reinforcing sentiments that prevail among parishioners, churches may be said to be influential in the sense that they exercise veto power or a braking force on major social change. Thus Seymour Martin Lipset argued that, precisely because church policy has generally remained in the political mainstream, churches have been a powerful force in American life, though more conservative than challenging:

> *Democratic and religious values have grown together. The results have been that, on the one hand, Americans see religion as essential to the support of the democratic institutions they cherish . . .; on the other hand, American denominations stress the ethical side of religion which they all have in common.*[32]

There are, however, cases in which the church and its ministry do run counter not only to prevailing societal sentiment but also to the views of parishioners. As the Campbell and Pettigrew analysis suggests, the perils of advocating an unpopular liberal position may be great, but advocacy of a conservative position can also pose a challenge when the status quo itself is eroding. The Catholic

---

[31] Quoted in Kenneth W. Underwood, *Protestant and Catholic* (Boston: Beacon Press, 1957), p. 106.

[32] Seymour Martin Lipset, *The First New Nation* (New York: Basic Books, 1963), p. 169.

position on birth control is such an instance in the present day. Catholicism continues to honor—even while it reconsidered—its traditional proscription against "artificial" birth control methods. Moreover, it has sought to realize its influence on society both directly on centers of power and indirectly via parishioners. Such a position, however, is increasingly at odds with newly promoted norms favoring birth control. The outcome is suggested by the results reported by Charles Westoff and Norman Ryder on three comparable surveys of 1955, 1960, and 1965 as part of the Growth of American Families series. Table 2 (see page 227) indicates that the proportion of Catholic women whose contraceptive practice conforms to Catholic doctrine has dropped off considerably during the ten years in which the new norms have risen to prominence. The pattern holds for both regular and less-frequent church attenders; and, as the researchers indicate elsewhere, conformity to church doctrine is especially low among younger Catholic wives and those with college education. Thus, the Catholic church's influence is waning, and the Pope's recent declaration may produce a major debacle. Still, several qualifications are needed before we leave the example. First, some Catholics continue to be affected (see the differences by rates of church attendance in Table 2; and it is true that Catholics continue to rank lower than Protestants in adopting new contraceptive practices). Second, even those Catholics who do use the newer techniques may still have larger families than Protestants because they actually choose to do so. Finally, even though Catholicism's indirect influence on society through its parishioners may be reduced, considerable *direct* influence remains. One of the ironies of the Catholic impact in this area is that it may well be greater on society at large than among Catholic parishioners alone. Because Catholics are the largest single denomination in

TABLE 2

Percentage of Catholic Women Conforming to Catholic
Doctrine on Contraception by Frequency of Church
Attendance: 1955, 1960, and 1965[a]

Year and Frequency of Church Attendance	ALL CATHOLIC WOMEN	
	Number of Women	Total Conforming
Total		
1955	787	70%
1960	668	62
1965	843	47
Regular[b]		
1955	533	78
1960	525	69
1965	607	56
Less Frequent		
1955	254	53
1960	143	35
1965	236	26

[a] Table reprinted from Charles F. Westoff and Norman B. Ryder, "United States: Methods of Fertility Control, 1955, 1960, and 1965," *Studies in Family Planning*, 17 (February 1967), 5.
[b] "Regular" means "regularly" in the 1955 and "once a week" in the 1960 survey to question on the frequency of attendance at religious services. In the 1965 survey the category means "once a week or more" to a question on attendance at mass.
SOURCE: Percentages for 1955 and 1960 adapted from Pascal K. Whelpton, Arthur A. Campbell, and John E. Patterson, *Fertility and Family Planning in the United States* (Princeton: Princeton Univ. Press, 1966), Table 160, p. 285.

America and because they are especially organized to fight bureaucratic fire with bureaucratic fire, Catholicism has considerable leverage as a pressure group. If one looks at recent legislative considerations of birth control, abortion, and divorce in such states as Wisconsin, Connecticut, Massachusetts, and New York, one perceives that Catholicism's direct political influence as an organized body is a major factor to be reckoned with, quite apart from the findings of recent statistical studies on the sentiments of Catholic parishioners.

So far, then, this discussion of the actual impact of religious organizations on the society has been confined to direct and indirect influence in rather conservative directions. Liberal impact, we suggested, is likely to resemble prophetic reinforcement if it emanates from local parishes; if it is to do more than reinforce, it is likely to come from nonparish sources. Actually, the source of such liberal sentiments is a major factor in determining their impact, and once again we are faced with the irony that the most prophetic facet of the church may be the least influential. After all, an important reason why radical statements emerge from nonparish situations is that they would not be supported by nonradical parishioners, the crucial soldiers in any religion's larger political battles.

In certain organizational forms, however, even radical messages can exert influence. We have just referred to the direct impact of the Catholic bureaucracy in the area of birth control, accenting the word "direct." Now it is time to accent the word "bureaucracy." Insofar as religion organizes to conduct information campaigns, to maintain lobbies in Washington and state capitols, and to carry on fund drives, it will have impact. These activities obviously are more easily carried out regionally than locally, nationally than regionally, and ecumenically than denominationally. Thus it is that the national headquarters of the Catholic church, the National Council of Churches, the National Conference of

Christians and Jews, the Southern Christian Leadership
Conference, and other organizations similarly composed
can move in the direction of their programs considerably
more effectively than can local parishes pushing for those
same programs. As with any lobby, the more money religion
can command, the more votes it can sway, the more pub-
licity it can attain, then the more persons for whom it is a
point of reference and the more power it has in local, state,
and national affairs.[33] Religion's influence in modern society, then, is neither pervasive and automatic (as in primitive society) nor hyperpolitical at the right hand of the elite
(as in premodern society). Instead, it is based upon the self-
conscious organization of its facilities into political instruments. And even such organization is no guarantee of
influence. Politics itself has increasingly turned away from
religion in any form as part of the differentiation of society.
Without arguing that religion has lost all influence, one can
argue that processes underway since the nineteenth century

---

[33] See R. Morton Darrow, "The Church and Techniques of Political
Action," in Smith and Jamison, *op. cit.*, pp. 161–193; and D. B.
Mayer, *The Protestant Search for Political Realism, 1919–1941*
(Berkeley: University of California Press, 1960). A very recent
account of organized religion's potency (and limitations) in the
political arena is found in Lee Rainwater and William L. Yancey
(eds.), *The Moynihan Report and the Politics of Controversy*
(Cambridge, Mass.: M.I.T. Press, 1967). Note, however, that
other institutions in American society illustrate the reverse trend.
As one crucial example, some have argued that the university has
suffered from "dedifferentiation" as it is increasingly drawn into
the orbit of the nation's major power centers. Thus, professors
speak out less but are listened to more. It is in this sense that C.
Wright Mills spoke of "knowledge as powerlessness," in a strategic
perversion of Lord Acton's axiom. Thus, as an intellectual becomes
recognized as a socially valuable expert, he becomes coopted into
the establishment for his utility and thereby loses his prophetic
independence. See Mills, *Power, Politics, and People*, ed. Irving
Louis Horowitz (New York: Ballantine Books, 1963), pp. 599–614.

have produced an attentuation in religious influence even while they have caused it to take new forms.

Summary

℧ It would be intimidating to try to assess the extent
℔ and condition of religious influence in contemporary society in twenty volumes, let alone twenty pages. Nevertheless, this chapter has sought to culminate the book by raising this most important of all issues. We have introduced a host of variables and a number of case studies, but there are a few particularly important themes that deserve reemphasis. Beginning with the assumption that our society has undergone increasing differentiation both within and between its major institutions, including religion, we took up two important religious functions for detailed consideration. In examining religion as a source of integration in society, we noted that the traditional church has been preempted to a very great extent by a "civil religion" that has the defects of its virtues in seeking to offer all things to all men. But the churches are also concerned to maximize integration and community within the parish setting itself. And this in turn leads to further considerations. For one thing, such an integrative role militates against vigorous pursuit of the second major religious function, that of religious prophecy in the interests of social change. There is a very real sense in which the functions of integration and prophecy are hostile to one another within the contemporary church. This is a major reason why the source of religious prophecy itself has shifted to nonparish personnel and to officials high in the church bureaucracies who have no specific parish flock to bind together.

However, one must distinguish between prophetic ventures and prophetic impact, and here a major irony is discernible. On the one hand, nonparish personnel are allowed to make prophetic pronouncements precisely because so few members of either their differentiated church or the differentiated society are affected; in a word, they are able to shout because so few are listening. On the other hand, the parish personnel are in the opposite situation. Because they are concerned over who will be listening, to the detriment of the parish's stability and membership, they are reluctant to shout and are confined to whispering. Both of these are responses to differentiation, though at different levels of the church organization. Neither offers a solution to the eclipse of religious influence in society. After all, is it better to maximize rhetoric without relevance or relevance at the price of prophetic rhetoric itself? Surely both options are far from optimal. In fact, the dilemma accounts for much of the agony as well as the joy of contemporary American religion.

But there is one last perspective that deserves a hearing. It may be that we are expecting too much in asking about the actual influence of religion on society's day-to-day events and policy decisions. It may be that we are overly sensitive to the lack of forceful impact. After all, one of the world's oldest axioms is that radical ideas suffer in the translation from ideology to practice. The very fact that contemporary religion is little involved in that translation may mean that it is better able to maintain its integrity in serving the no less valuable function of providing new insights and nurturing older truths beyond the arena of politics. Certainly this chapter has not meant to suggest that religion has lost all its roles in contemporary society. This last role not only has been increasing, but may be the most important in the long run. Any complex society runs the risk of becoming too complex to ponder its course and destiny in a niche removed from the bureaucratic marketplace. To that extent, every society may depend upon a relationship with religion that resembles the one now forming in our own society today.

SELECTED ANNOTATED BIBLIOGRAPHY

The following list of books and articles is not intended to be exhaustive. It offers instead a mixture of classic and current works that are recommended for those who want to read further. Each work, of course, points to others, and we have tried to pick those that will stimulate readers to follow their leads rather than tax readers to the extent of giving up altogether.

Allport, Gordon W. *The Individual and His Religion.* New York: Macmillan, 1950. A discussion of the psychology of religion, including a number of functions religion may serve for the individual personality.

Bellah, Robert N. "Civil Religion in America," *Daedalus,* 96 (Winter 1967), 1–21. A brief but excellent identification of the system of "religious" beliefs located in and around the federal government.

————. "Religious Evolution," *American Sociological Review,* 29 (June 1964), 358–374. This neoevolutionary orientation toward social change discusses the sequential stages of differentiation through which Western religious institutions have gone.

Berger, Peter. *The Sacred Canopy.* New York: Doubleday, 1967. The functions of religion seen from the perspective of the sociology of knowledge and the psychology of meaning, all within the historical framework of the West.

Bouquet, A. C. *Comparative Religion.* London: Penguin Books, 1941. Though only one of several good summary descriptions of the world's religions, Bouquet's is very readable, short, and a paperback.

Clark, Elmer T. *The Small Sects in America.* Rev. ed. Nashville: Abingdon Press, 1949. A description of the numerous small sects and cults, giving information on their history, theological beliefs, and membership. The book is exotic, if somewhat dated in its statistics.

Douglass, H. Paul, and Edmund de S. Brunner. *The Protestant Church as a Social Institution.* New York: Harper & Row, 1935. Interesting largely as an early effort in the empirical, quantitative study of religious organizations.

Durkheim, Emile. *The Elementary Forms of the Religious Life.* Trans. J. W. Swain. New York: Free Press, 1947. One of the undisputed classics in the sociological investigation of religion, *The Elementary Forms* raises questions of the social effects as well as the causes of religious behavior in the context of primitive society and totemism.

Festinger, Leon, Henry W. Riecken, Jr., and Stanley Schachter. *When Prophecy Fails.* New York: Harper Torchbooks, 1965. Here participant observation in an apocalyptic sect produces a fascinating narrative of the development of both a particular religious group and a more general theory of individual religious involvement.

Fichter, Joseph H., S.J., *Religion as an Occupation: A Study in the Sociology of Professions.* Notre Dame: University of Notre Dame Press, 1961. One of the few large-scale discussions of religious professionals, though most materials are restricted to Roman Catholicism.

Freud, Sigmund. *The Future of an Illusion.* Trans. W. D. Robson-Scott. Garden City, N.Y.: Anchor Books, 1964. A considerably broadened Freudian explanation, published first in 1927, wherein Freud concentrates more on ever-present "causes" of religion.

————. *Totem and Taboo.* Trans. A. A. Brill. New York: Vintage, 1960. First published in 1913, representing an early effort to "explain" the origin of religion.

Glenn, Norval D., and Ruth Hyland. "Religious Preference and Worldly Success: Some Evidence from National Surveys," *American Sociological Review,* 32 (February 1967), 73–86. A careful and extensive evaluation of religious differences according to recent public opinion poll data. The Weber thesis is unsubstantiated, suggesting that Weber was right in denying that it would continue to be confirmed.

Glock, Charles Y., and Rodney Stark. *Religion and Society in Tension.* Chicago: Rand McNally, 1965. A collection of essays that not only reveals many of the distinctions with which Glock has become associated but also uses those distinctions to point up religious paradoxes in the present day.

Glock, Charles Y., Benjamin B. Ringer, and Earl R. Babbie. *To Comfort and to Challenge.* Berkeley: University of California Press, 1967. Based on a survey of Episcopalian clergy and parishioners, this book analyzes the paradox in religious organizations between their desire to change people and their desire to provide solace and support.

Goode, William J. *Religion Among the Primitives*. New York: Free Press, 1951. A good example of contemporary theorizing from primitive materials about religion's interinstitutional relationships.

Greeley, Andrew M., and Peter H. Rossi. *The Education of Catholic Americans*. Chicago: Aldine, 1966. A rigorous examination of the effects of Catholic versus non-Catholic schooling on such Weberian variables as secular achievements and aspirations. Here, too, the conclusions suggest that the Weber thesis is not applicable today, if indeed it ever was.

Harrison, Paul M. *Authority and Power in the Free Church Tradition: A Social Case Study of the American Baptist Convention*. Princeton, N.J.: Princeton University Press, 1959. An organizational analysis identifying the "subversion" of some traditional religious goals as a result of pursuing more instrumental ends.

Herberg, Will. *Protestant, Catholic, Jew*. Garden City, N.Y.: Anchor Books, 1960. One of the best-known essays in the sociology of American religion, Herberg's thesis argues that the three religious groups have moved closer together, serving now as alternative ways of "being American."

James, William. *The Varieties of Religious Experience*. New York: Mentor, 1958. A classic from one of America's intellectual giants, this treatment introduces the famed distinction between religions of the "sick soul" and religions of the "healthy-minded."

Johnson, Benton. "Theology and the Position of Pastors on Public Issues," *American Sociological Review*, 32 (June 1967), 433–442. An empirical analysis of the effects of theology upon political ideology, together with a sophisticated attempt to account for the relationships uncovered.

Lenski, Gerhard. *The Religious Factor*. Garden City, N.Y.: Doubleday, 1961. One of the few elaborate, multivariate analyses of religious behavior in contemporary American society.

Malinowski, Bronislaw. *Magic, Science, and Religion and Other Essays*. Garden City, N.Y.: Anchor Books, 1955. A classic analysis of forces producing religion and magical practices in preliterate societies.

Marx, Gary T. "Religion: Opiate or Inspiration of Civil Rights Militancy Among Negroes?" *American Sociological Review*, 32

(February 1967), 64–73. Empirical confirmation of the suspected negative relation between religious and civil rights involvement among Negroes, though it makes a difference what sort of religion is at issue.

May, Henry F. *Protestant Churches and Industrial America.* New York: Harper & Row, 1949. A masterful historical account of the firing of twentieth-century Protestantism in the forge of nineteenth-century social and economic change. The book suggests that the awakening of the churches was too little and too late.

Meyer, Donald B. *The Protestant Search for Political Realism, 1919–1941.* Berkeley: University of California Press, 1960. A study of Protestant churches' developing awareness of political methods for pursuing their aims, revolving largely around the early career of the theologian Reinhold Niebuhr.

Niebuhr, H. Richard. *The Social Sources of Denominationalism.* New York: Holt, Rinehart and Winston, 1929. A historical and sociological treatment of a number of forces causing Protestant Christianity to separate into many groups.

Norbeck, Edward. *Religion in Primitive Society.* New York: Harper & Row, 1961. A good summary of a great many ethnographic accounts of religion in preliterate societies.

Pope, Liston. *Millhands and Preachers.* 2nd ed. New Haven, Conn.: Yale University Press, 1965. A fascinating account of the pressures on clergymen in a cotton mill town to take sides on labor-management disputes during the Depression. The second edition contains an introductory essay by R. A. Peterson and N. J. Demerath III identifying a number of key theoretical issues to which Pope's monograph is related.

Robertson Smith, W. *Lectures on the Religion of the Semites.* Rev. ed. London: Adam and Charles Black, 1901. A major work that had great influence on Durkheim's theory of religion, owing largely to Robertson Smith's attention to the interrelationships between religion and the political order.

Samuelsson, Kurt. *Religion and Economic Action: A Critique of Max Weber.* New York: Harper Torchbooks, 1964. A succinct —and devastating—critique of the particulars in Weber's thesis regarding the role of the Protestant Ethic in the rise of economic rationality.

Sklare, Marshall. *Conservative Judaism.* New York: Free Press, 1955. A historical analysis of that branch of Judaism which is uniquely American, this study anticipated Herberg's account of the role of generations of immigrants in modifying American religion.

Smith, Charles Merrill. *How to Become a Bishop Without Being Religious.* Garden City, N.Y.: Doubleday, 1965. Trenchant satire that illuminates painlessly what many sociologists have said so painfully.

Smith, J. W., and A. L. Jamison (eds.) *Religion in American Life.* 2 vols. Princeton, N.J.: Princeton University Press, 1961. Of mixed quality, the essays contained in these volumes nevertheless range widely over the roots and consequences of American religion.

Swanson, Guy E. *The Birth of the Gods.* Ann Arbor: University of Michigan Press, 1960. Durkheimian ground covered with empirical turf; an attempt to apply survey techniques in an analysis of some fifty preliterate societies and their religious systems.

Troeltsch, Ernst. *The Social Teaching of the Christian Churches.* 2 vols. Trans. Olive Wyon. New York: Harper Torchbooks, 1960. Lengthy descriptions of developing Christianity by one of Weber's students in which the latter's ideas regarding church-sect differences are elaborated. Beyond this feature, Troeltsch shows the relationship between theological ideas and resulting organizational forms.

Underwood, Kenneth W. *Protestant and Catholic.* Boston: Beacon Press, 1957. An analysis of the role of churches in one community's conflict over a planned-parenthood campaign.

Wach, Joachim. *Sociology of Religion.* Chicago: University of Chicago Press, 1944. The first American text in the sociology of religion, distinguishable for its coverage of details and descriptions of theoretically pertinent periods in Western history.

Weber, Max. *The Protestant Ethic and the Spirit of Capitalism.* Trans. Talcott Parsons. New York: Scribner, 1928; paperback ed. 1958. A thesis regarding changes in Western religion and subsequent changes in the economic sphere. The reverberations of this work are heard not only in sociology of religion but also in economic history, philosophy, and political science.

———. *The Sociology of Religion.* Trans. Ephraim Fischoff. Boston: Beacon Press, 1963. Though Weber's thoughts about religion are scattered throughout his work (including, besides *The Protestant Ethic and the Spirit of Capitalism, Ancient Judaism, The Religion of India,* and *The Religion of China*), this volume brings many of them together into Weber's most systematic statement.

Wilson, Bryan R. "An Analysis of Sect Development," *American Sociological Review,* 24 (February 1959), 3–15. A recent and systematic effort to classify small religious groups so as to account for their varying propensities to become large and bureaucratic.

Yinger, J. Milton. *Religion in the Struggle for Power*. Durham, N.C.: Duke University Press, 1946. An insightful analysis of the paradoxes confronting religion as it is organized to further many aims, including the aim of influencing society.

INDEX